SUPERCONS
THROUGH M

to/ Dan,

Best Wishes
on your Birthday,

Love Pat (1983)
XXX

Also by Dr Baker

ANTHROPOGENY
ESOTERIC ANATOMY
ESOTERIC ASTROLOGY
ESOTERIC HEALING
ESOTERIC PSYCHOLOGY
THE JEWEL IN THE LOTUS
THE OPENING OF THE THIRD EYE
POWERS LATENT IN MAN
PRACTICAL TECHNIQUES OF ASTRAL PROJECTION
THE PSYCHOLOGY OF DISCIPLESHIP
THE SEVEN RAYS
THE THEORY AND PRACTICE OF MEDITATION

SUPERCONSCIOUSNESS THROUGH MEDITATION

by

Dr DOUGLAS BAKER
B.A., M.R.C.S., L.R.C.P., F.Z.S.

and

CELIA HANSEN, B.A., M.A.

THE AQUARIAN PRESS
Wellingborough, Northamptonshire

First published 1978
Second Impression 1979

ISBN 0 85030 152 1 (UK)
ISBN 0 87728 384 2 (USA)

Photoset in Great Britain by
Specialised Offset Services Ltd, Liverpool
and printed and bound in Great Britain

Contents

Part One

The Biology of Spiritual Development

You ask, how can we know the Infinite? I answer, not by reason. It is the office of reason to distinguish and define. The Infinite, therefore, cannot be ranked among its objects. You can only apprehend the Infinite by a faculty superior to reason, by entering into a state in which you are your finite self no longer – in which the divine essence is communicated to you. This is ecstasy. It is the liberation of your mind from its finite consciousness. Like can only apprehend like; when you thus cease to be finite, you become one with the infinite. In the reduction of your soul to its simplest self, its divine essence, you realize this union, this identity.

Plotinus: *Letter to Flaccus*

1
Ancient Mysteries

Cosmic Consciousness

The goal of all major esoteric traditions and of all world religions is entry into a higher kingdom of nature, into the realm of the gods. This kingdom is known as the Fifth Kingdom, and one's awareness and experience of this world constitute what is referred to as the 'superconscious experience'. It has been described by all those who have had this extraordinary glimpse of another world, in ecstatic terms, as a state of boundless being and bliss in which one's individual consciousness merges with the universal consciousness, with the Godhead. It is a state of beingness and awareness that far surpasses one's usual limited, narrow view of reality and transports one, for a brief moment, beyond the limits of time and space into another dimension.

The union of the self in man with the Self of the universe is called yoga, the yoking or joining together of the finite self with the Infinite Self, and the process or method for attaining this union is also called yoga.

The name given by the Hindus to the highest state of consciousness is called 'Samadhi'; the Zen Buddhists refer to it as 'Satori'; in Taoism it is known as 'the absolute Tao'. Thomas Merton calls it 'transcendental unconscious', while the Quakers label it the 'Inner Light', and Gurdjieff calls it 'objective consciousness'. Jung describes it as the process of individuation, and in Western metaphysical traditions it is called the 'fifth state', 'cosmic consciousness', 'illumination', and 'the mystical or religious experience'.

No matter what name is given to this phenomenon, the condition implies a state of awareness radically different from that of our ordinary normal waking consciousness. These terms are all descriptive of the merging or union of individual consciousness with that of a Greater Being and becoming one with Him. When this occurs, there is really no loss of individuality or sense of annihilation, but rather an expansion into a greater beingness in which you discover that, although 'you are your finite self no longer', you are something far more glorious than you can ever imagine and that the loss of your finite self is really no loss at all. In fact, it is not, as is stated in the famous line, that the 'dewdrop slips into the Shining Sea', but rather that the dewdrop becomes the Shining Sea.

In order to achieve this extraordinary state of awareness and beingness, many disciplines and methods have been developed over the centuries, both by religion and by esoteric traditions known as mystery schools. Only those who proved themselves worthy and who could be trusted were permitted to enter these schools and be given the keys with which to unlock the hidden potentials within, for the misuse of this information could lead to dire consequences both to themselves and to others. Even the world's great religions had information which was withheld from the masses and reserved for those few who had earned the right to have this knowledge.

The Mystery Schools

It is a little known fact that every ancient religion and philosophical system had an esoteric[1] or secret teaching for the select few, while there was an exoteric or public teaching for the masses. These ancient teachings, which are known as 'The Mysteries', dealt with the great Truths about the nature of Reality and of being and non-being. Among other things, the Mysteries included in their teachings the study of the

[1] Esoteric – the word has a two-fold meaning: (1) knowledge held in secret, known only to a few and (2) secrets concealed from mankind by nature.

origin of the cosmos, called Cosmogenesis, and the study of the origin of man, known as Anthropogenesis. Needless to say, these views differ somewhat from those introduced later by modern science and by present-day theology.

In the world of the ancient civilizations of Egypt, Greece, India, Caledonia, and Somothrace, there existed the 'greater' (secret) mysteries and the 'lesser' (public) mysteries. The priests of those days, from the Hierophants of Egypt to the Bhramins of India, and later the Hebrew Rabbis, kept their inner teachings hidden from the public for fear that they would profane and distort this sacred knowledge. The Jewish Rabbis called their outer religious ceremonies 'The Mercavah', meaning the exterior body, the vehicle or covering which contains the hidden soul, i.e., the highest teaching. Today their esoteric teaching is preserved in the form of the Kabala. Then we have the celebrated public rituals known as the Eleusinia in Greece, and the 'greater' and 'lesser' teachings of Northern Buddhism, known respectively as the Mahayana, the esoteric school, and Hinayana, the exoteric school of Buddhism. Pythagoras preserved the higher teachings for his pledged disciples only, binding them by oath to secrecy and silence.

In Egypt, the initiated priests developed occult alphabets and secret ciphers for their pledged disciples to preserve their ancient wisdom. It is interesting to note that the Tarot cards which are so popular today are said to contain the key to the Egyptian mysteries. Even in the history of early Christianity we find the inner teachings preserved for the initiated, while the husks, the outer 'vehicle' were given to the public. 'To you', said Christ, speaking to his disciples, 'it is given to know the mysteries of the kingdom of heaven; but unto them that are without all these things are done in parables.'[2] And in the Bible, what is recorded are the parables of Jesus, but the 'mysteries of the kingdom' are withheld.

Today, the mystery schools are no longer in existence, and the world's religions possess only a fraction of this

[2] Mark 4:11

information. Whatever vestiges of such knowledge that remain in religious teachings have been distorted into a meaningless dogma and ritual which is little understood by the common man and which has only served to separate mankind to a greater extent than before. The separateness occurs because of the disagreements which have arisen in the understanding and interpretation of scriptures produced by individuals who have had the superconscious experience. Those who have not had this experience would, of course, interpret it in terms of their level of understanding based on their own experiences in our limited three-dimensional world. Unfortunately, all religions that are known to us in their church form are only 'pseudo-religions' and present only a travesty of the great Truths.

The question arises, then, if esoteric knowledge exists, where can it be found? The answer, of course, is that the true science of spiritual development always lay in the hands of the Masters of the Wisdom who constitute the inner circle of humanity and who guide the evolution of mankind on this planet. All that is possible is done by them to help man, but he must seek help. Moreover, he must first understand that there is a knowledge that far surpasses all ordinary knowledge and that the only way to gain access to that knowledge is to seek it through contact with the Masters.

But man, when faced with the idea of a hidden knowledge that would change him from ordinary man into a god, largely ignores it, and those who do hear the call of the Pied Piper get lost in the cul-de-sac of psychism and pseudo-esotericism because they themselves do not know what they are looking for, and in order to receive, one must know what to look for. Clearly, esoteric knowledge can be given only to those who seek it, for in order to acquire this knowledge and the power that accompanies it, one must go through many preparations, tests, and hard work.

Spiritual Development

The science of spiritual development is acknowledged to be one of the most difficult of all tasks that man voluntarily sets himself because he has to search for heaven with the properties of heaven itself. For in order to find the realm wherein the qualities of Love and Compassion exist, we have to manifest such qualities in ourselves first. In other words, we must be able to cultivate these attitudes and virtues so that they become a part of our very nature. That is why in the teachings of all esoteric traditions, we have the moral and ethical injuctions placed first, before methods and techniques are given to accelerate the snail-like pace of evolution. In Raja Yoga – the classical system of meditation that is set forth in the Yoga Sutras of Patanjali – we find the Yamas (the five abstentions), and the Niyamas (the five observances), listed as Steps 1 and 2 of the eightfold limbs of yoga that lead to Samadhi, the superconscious experience.

Practising this method or that technique alone does not – in and of itself – bring about spiritual growth and unfoldment or ensure entry into the fifth kingdom. Many false advertisements and claims abound promising quick results in meditation and the unfoldment of psychic abilities and powers without including these moral and ethical codes of conduct. Some individuals, because they have temporarily activated a chakra through some method, begin to have psychic experiences, and they naively believe that they are making 'spiritual' progress, when, in fact, growth and unfoldment have not occurred at all. What they have acquired are pseudo-gifts which are of a temporary nature.

The real Siddhis (powers) are a by-product of spiritual unfoldment, and in the Yoga Sutras of Patanjali we are warned not to make the psychic powers the primary focus, as we can be diverted from the goal of self-realization. When, however, these powers develop one may use them in service to humanity, with complete detachment and dispassion. Progress in spiritual unfoldment is first registered in the disciple as increased ability to manage his daily affairs, increased responsibility to handle his portion of the Plan of the Planetary Logos,[3] elimination as the Soul's purpose is

[3] Logos – the Greater Being in which we all live, and move, and have our Being. See Postulate 2 in Douglas Baker's *The Jewel in the Lotus*.

allowed to express itself,[4] and a growing awareness, understanding, and expansion of consciousness of Life itself.

[4] See *Esoteric Healing* (Volume One) by Douglas Baker. 'After 25 years of patient research in the ways of Orthodox Medicine and its esoteric counterpart, I have no reason to change my firm belief that the cause of ninety per cent of all disease lies in the inability of Man to express himself according to the purposes of his own Soul whether he be aware of these purposes or not.'

2
Building the Bridgehead

The Antakarana

The essence of spiritual development is that we need to build a bridgehead between the Soul and the personality to establish communication between the Soul and its lower vehicle. This bridgehead is called 'The Antakarana' in Sanscrit and is described as a channel along which the energy of the Soul flows with ever-increasing force into the energy vortices of the body known as chakras. In average man only five per cent of the soul's energies are available to him, but through the practice of meditation he begins to establish a bridgehead, to build the Antakarana or Jacob's ladder. The diagram on page 16 illustrates the bridgehead that is constructed between the soul and the personality vehicle. When the Soul is functioning completely within the personality, we have what is known as the 'soul-infused personality'.

Consider the space rockets of man for a moment. Each rocket contains part of our culture, our science. In the carefully adjusted radio-signals that bleep from the rocket, hover the ghosts of Edison and Marconi. In the flash of its departure lie the efforts of Rutherford, of Dalton, of Oliver Lodge. In the mathematically calculated course it takes, is the skill of Kepler, the perception of Galileo, the intuition of Isaac Newton, as well as the geometry of Euclid and Pythagoras.

It is all there – our greatest efforts duplicated and re-duplicated in the workings of the rocket – the struggles of root races, the rise and fall of dynasties, the shackling and

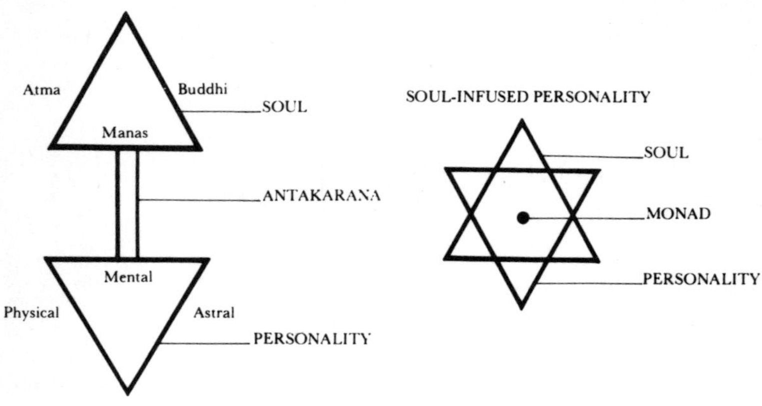

1. Bridgehead Between Soul and Personality Vehicle.

unshackling of religions, the freeing of sciences, Hargreaves, Coulomb, Watt, and Stevenson! Their mental deposits lie in our rockets as surely as their transmitted chromosomes lie in many of us. And what do we do with this product of our ingenuity? We shoot it out into space, probably never to see it again. Each rocket improves on the next and the grasp out into space becomes firmer and longer, like a plant shooting upwards – a sort of antakarana.

The same occurs in man. After reaching a certain stage of spiritual development, we eventually begin to use our finest energies to build a bridgehead out into inner space – or rather 'upwards'. This is the science of Yoga, the yoking of the lower man with the infinite which lies in inner space. The many techniques for procuring this growth in man, of his flowering into perfection, lie in such processes as meditation, in one-pointed concentration, in relaxation, and in breathing. The projection of ourselves into inner space has been successfully achieved by many before us and their records constitute the Wisdom of the Ages of which the esoteric sciences are but a part.

Example from Nature

The path to self-unfoldment and adeptship is always best illustrated from nature, for all of nature is moving towards perfection. The four kingdoms of nature are in various stages of evolution. For example, the vegetable kingdom is flowering into perfection. We are surrounded everywhere by examples of its radiance and adeptship. The mineral kingdom, on the other hand, has hardly, as yet, evolved except for the glorious jewels and the semi-precious stones which represent their highest lives in their spiritual stream. While the animal kingdom is more advanced than mineral, it lags behind man and the vegetable kingdom. Man is relatively less advanced in the journey of the kingdoms toward their goal of perfection than the plant kingdom, though way ahead of the other two. However, this does not imply that plants are more advanced beings than humans, for all the lives within plants have yet to reach the human stage.

However, by studying the flowering plants, we can observe, by analogy, what may well be the process for ourselves, and we can gain an understanding of our own spiritual path preceding initiaion[1] into a flowering man or adept. If you had walked this planet 90 million years ago, you would not have seen a flower; you would have seen only green plants. What a miracle it would have been for you if you had looked at a green plant and suddenly seen it swell at its meristem, and after a point of great tension and crisis burst open into a glorious flower! Actually, the angiosperms burst suddenly upon the world and evolution only about 75 million years ago...a suddenness that still confounds the evolutionists. Their arrival signalled the fact that some parts of the plant kingdom were reaching the climax of their spiritual evolution in the plant kingdom and were ready for initiation.

An analogy may be drawn between the search of man into

[1] Initiation is the process of undergoing an expansion of consciousness through the application of the rod of initiation by the Planetary Logos, for no man can initiate you. Also, these initiations take place on the inner planes.

inner and outer space and the final flowering. In the case of the plant, the seed, which is thrust into the fertile soil, contains within it all the potentialities of its previous lives or antecedents. When conditions are right, the seed will send out roots. The level of the ground is the barrier between inner and outer space – the hard earth and the subtler air and sunlight. All the time that the plant is searching with its roots for nutrition, it is growing and building up energy. Later, there is an unfoldment of itself in the subtler (inner) realm of the atmosphere and the leaves begin to absorb a different energy – the energy of sunlight. As it begins to flower, its scent increases its 'Ring-Pass-Not'[2] enormously. The colours of the flowering perfection are unbelievably beautiful when compared with the drab green of the mere plant before it flowered.

The correspondence in man is the sending out of the monadic seed from the flame divine into matter. Many lives are spent gathering all the energies and lessons of lives devoted to material experience. Like the plant that begins to thrust itself into the atmosphere to absorb the energy of the sunlight, so too man puts out a part of himself, the antakarana, into inner space and draws on the inner energies. These build up until there is a veritable bud of energy of higher nature. Finally, after stress and struggle, the bud begins to open and man unfolds his inner nature. When this occurs, qualities undreamed of begin to radiate from him as they do in the plant when it begins to flower. His 'Ring-Pass-Not' also increases as he contacts dimensions of awareness not previously accessible to him.

The point of importance to remember is the upper and lower nature of the plant and of man and the interconnecting antakarana which has to be built by the lower plant or man. The biology of spiritual development is concerned with the cultivation and watering of this human tree. Cultivation is

[2] Ring-Pass-Not – the circle, bounds or frontier beyond which an entity cannot go because of the limitations of its state of consciousness.

through exercises of discipline; watering is through instructions of initiates who give out the ancient teachings on its development. As we enter the Age of Aquarius, we can perceive the true meaning of the symbol for the zodiacal sign of Aquarius which depicts a man bearing a jug of water that is being poured forth watering the tree of mankind.

The Chakras

A further analogy of man resembling a flowering plant can be made with regard to the chakras or lotuses located in the etheric tract along the spinal column. There are seven major centres, and although we are most familiar with the chakras that lie in the etheric sheath, the astral and mental sheaths also possess a set of seven chakras each. However, the chakras that we are concerned with here are the ones lying along the etheric tract in the spinal column. Ordinarily they are not visible to the physical eye, but any particular centre can be seen clairvoyantly when that centre is activated.

However, we need to have a correct understanding of what constitutes chakras or force centres. Symbolically speaking, chakras are cosmic banks. Every real effort that we make, every effort that has a right motive, whether it is successful or not, brings a deposit of some record inside these chakras. So when succeeding lives come, when we re-incarnate, the qualities we have deposited in these chakras are quickly restored to us and we reach that same level of achievement that we had before. In each life, we start off with the rewards gained in previous lives, because every act of Atma, Buddhi and Manas[3] is a sparkling jewel placed in these cosmic banks. Likewise, in those lives that lie ahead, these cosmic banks are available to us. When sufficient development has taken place in these chakras, man awakens to a new awareness of himself and of the world which was not present before the awakening and which is beyond the range of detection of his physical senses.

[3] Atma, Buddhi, Manas, represent the qualities of the Higher Triad, Will, Love-wisdom, and Active Intelligence.

The chakras, which literally mean 'circles' or 'wheels' in Sanscrit, are connected to their physical counterparts, the endocrine glands and the nerve plexuses, through an extensive system of channels called nadis along which Prana, cosmic energy, is conveyed from the centres to the organs of the physical body. It is Prana which is responsible for the maintenance of life in the physical body. While oxygen and carbon are absorbed directly by the physical body through respiration, Prana, the energy globule attached to the oxygen molecule, is absorbed by the etheric body and channelled through the physical body through the system of nadis. Furthermore, while oxygen cannot be stored in the body, Prana can be stored.

The Nadis

There are three major channels or nadis which are considered primary: Ida, Pingala, and Sushumna. (*See Diagram*). The central channel, sushumna, extends from the Muladhara Chakra, at the base of the spine, to the Ajna Chakra, the

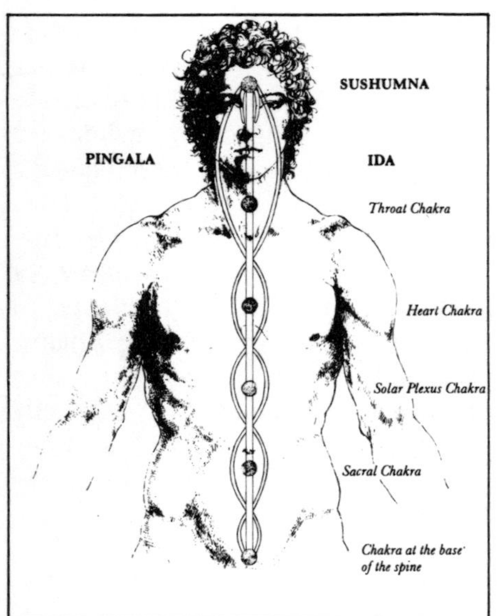

2. The Three Major Nadis.

centre between the eyebrows, while Ida and Pingala are connected to the left and right nostrils respectively and intertwine Sushumna Nadi in a serpentine pattern. Each of these nadis extends from Muladhara Chakra to Ajna Chakra, meeting sushumna at each of these chakras. In Hatha Yoga, the nadi known as pingala begins in the right nostril and is represented by the symbol of the sun; it has a positive polarity and is referred to as Ha. The nadi beginning in the left nostril is represented by the symbol of the moon; it has a negative polarity and is referred to as Tha. This is, in fact, the origin of the word Hatha, referring to the disciplines of that particular branch of yoga.

It is interesting to note that references to solar and lunar energies are also found in the Ancient Greek and Egyptian Mystery Schools. According to these teachings the passage of energies into sushumna and the activation of the chakras takes place in only five of the force centres and is called the 'Lunar Cycle'. The Greeks referred to this cycle as the 'Journey of the Moon', as it symbolized the purificatory period on the path of self-unfoldment. Accordingly, the Higher Awakening takes place with the descent of solar fire from above which vivifies all seven of the centres and is called the 'Solar Cycle' or the 'Journey of the Sun'. It must be noted that we are not speaking of the passage of kundalini fire into the central channel, as this takes place at a later stage in the individual's development.

Although prana is continuously circulating through ida and pingala, it does not circulate through the central channel, sushumna. In ordinary man, the entrance to sushumna nadi at the base of the spine is closed and remains closed throughout his life. When, however, through practice of esoteric disciplines and purification the prana is withdrawn from ida and pingala and enters sushumna at the Muladhara Chakra, the practice of concentration and meditation can be undertaken to a greater advantage. The reason for this is that when the positive and negative currents of ida and pingala are brought together in sushumna, they are neutralized, and it is then possible to still the body, breath, and mind. In light of this, Patanjali's definition of Yoga becomes more meaningful, for in the second sutra, he defines Yoga as 'the inhibition of the modifications of the mind'. In other words, Yoga (union) is possible when we have succeeded in stilling the thought waves in the mind.

The manner in which the nadis join at the various centres gives the appearance of lotuses with petals. The petals increase in number as they ascend the spine. (*See Diagram*)

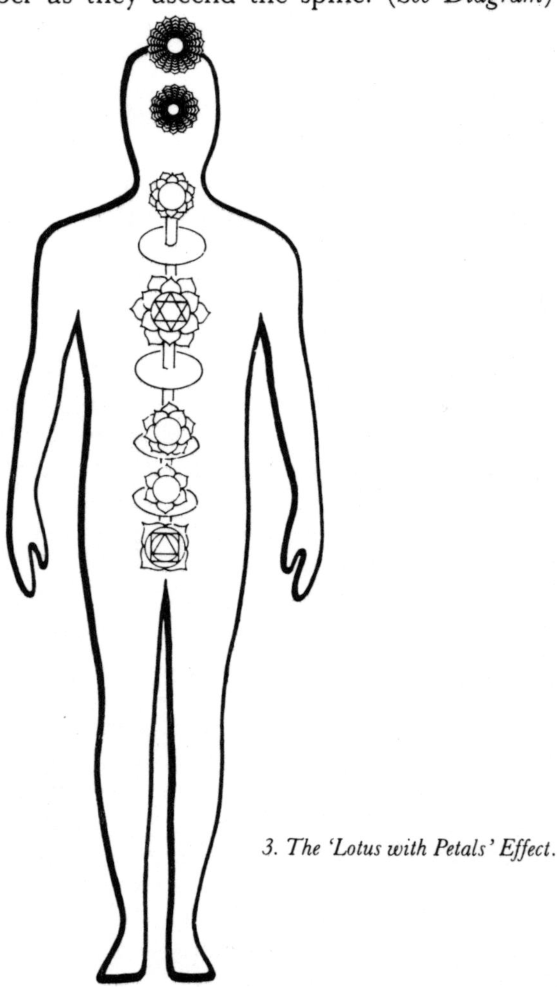

3. The 'Lotus with Petals' Effect.

The true lotus flower contains within it, in embryo, the whole structure of the adult plant into which it will grow. Lotus flowers have their roots in the mud of the pool. The stem grows upwards out of the mud (Earth) through the water (Emotions) into the air (Mentality). The chakras not only evolve or unfold, like the flower, through the welter of physical, emotional, and mental experiences in many lives, but they also contain within them the latent or embryonic possibilities of man. As they open, the latent powers in man unfold.

Each of the chakras has a certain number of petals assigned to it ranging from two to a thousand, and each petal is inscribed with a letter of the sanscrit alphabet for awakening the chakra through Mantra Yoga.[4] In addition, each of the chakras has certain characteristics assigned to it which include geometric form, element or tattva, dominant colour, inherent sound, type of power, and controlling deities. The geometric forms and colours of the centres are universal and are found in all esoteric traditions. For example, the geometric form, which is called a yantra in Sanscrit, as well as the colour and element, are basically the same in both the Hindu system and in the Kabala, the Jewish mystical system for the inner development of man.

However, the other characteristics that distinguish each chakra such as the presiding deities, are purely Hindu in character. Therefore, when performing the visualization exercise called Chakra Dharana[5] to develop concentration, one may use a symbol that corresponds to the quality expressed by that chakra. Thus, for the Muladhara Chakra that is presided over by the elephant deity Ganesha, we can substitute the image of the rhinoceros, the symbol of blind power; this is indeed true of the quality of the energy of this chakra.

[4] Mantra Yoga, the science of sound vibration, based on the principle that everything is in vibration and therefore the sounding of certain sounds produces an effect on the human being and his environment.

[5] Dharana, Sanscrit word for concentration.

In visualizing the throat chakra, the higher creative centre in man, and therefore, the alter ego of the sacral centre, the Westerner could use the symbol of a camel, which represents the factor of lower mind, as this chakra incorporates the qualities of the Third Ray[6] of Active Intelligence. By visualising the throat chakra and its symbols, energy from the sacral centre is transferred to the throat. It must be remembered that the process of yoga involves the transference of energies from chakras below the diaphragm to those above it, until all of the energies are centred in the head region. When this occurs, the thousand lotus blooms in the crown chakra, man is liberated from matter, and a fire god is born.

Symbolism of the Chakras

1. Muladhara, at the base of the spine; Yantra, a yellow square representing Prithivi, the element earth; the Bija Mantra[7] is Lam (physical correspondence, Adrenal Glands).
2. Svadhisthana, sacral centre, second vertebrae above the coccyx; Yantra, a silver crescent moon representing Apas, the element of water, the Bija Mantra is Vam (physical correspondence, Gonads of male and female reproductive system).
3. Manipura, solar plexus centre, at the level of the navel in the spine; Yantra, a red triangle, apex down, representing Tejas, the element of fire, the Bija Mantra is Ram; (physical correspondence, solar plexus and pancreas).
4. Anahata, heart centre, at the level of the heart in the spine; Yantra, a blue hexagram formed by two interlacing triangles giving the appearance of a six-pointed star, representing Vayu, the element of air; the Bija Mantra is Yam (physical correspondence, thymus gland).
5. Vishuddha, throat centre, at the throat; Yantra, a dark indigo oval egg or a white circle within a triangle, apex down, representing Akasha, the element of ether; the Bija Mantra is Ham; (physical correspondence, thyroid gland).

[6] See *Esoteric Psychology* (Volume Five) by Douglas Baker, for a full study and understanding of the Seven Rays.
[7] The Bija Mantra, pronounced Bej, is the inherent sound, note, or seed syllable of the chakra.

6. Ajna, brow centre, between the eyebrows; Yantra, a golden sun representing Mahat, the element of Cosmic Mind; The Bija Mantra is Ksham (k is silent); (physical correspondence, pituitary gland).
7. Sahasrara, crown centre, top of the head; Yantra, a scintillating white thousand-petalled lotus with a blue centre, the element is beyond all elements and the colour is beyond all colours; the Bija Mantra is OM (physical correspondence, pineal gland).

The visualization of the yantras, i.e., the geometric shapes with their corresponding colours, and the sounding of the Bija Mantra, the note of the chakra, while meditating on the quality inherent in each chakra, prepares the centre for activation. Eventually, after long practice, together with the adherence to other esoteric disciplines, including purification, one achieves mastery over each of the elements, as well as knowledge and mastery of the plane of consciousness corresponding to the particular chakra. The function of each of the etheric centres – when fully aroused – is to bring into physical consciousness whatever may be the quality inherent in the astral centre which corresponds to it.

Thus, when the solar plexus centre, Manipura Chakra, comes into activity, one begins to become conscious of all kinds of astral influences, friendly or hostile. With the opening of the heart centre, Anahata Chakra, man becomes instinctively aware of the joys and sorrows of others and sometimes even causes him to sympathetically reproduce their aches and pains. The opening of the throat chakra, Vishudda, allows one to hear voices and eventually leads to clairaudience, while the opening of the brow centre, Ajna Chakra, enables one to see things and to have various waking visions of people and places. The full opening of this chakra brings clairvoyance. However, the activation of this chakra is not be be confused with the awakening of the third eye which is an organ that emerges with the interplay of the three major chakras, Brow, Crown, and Alta Major Centres.[8] Finally,

[8] See *The Opening of the Third Eye* by Douglas Baker.

when the Crown Chakra, the thousand-petalled lotus, is fully aroused, man has the ability to leave the body and to return to it at will. It also brings continuity of consciousness even at death.

CHAKRA CHART I

CHAKRA	**YANTRA**	**ELEMENT**	**COLOUR**	**BIJA MANTRA**
Muladhara (Base of spine)	Square	Earth	Yellow	LAM
Svadhisthana (Sacral Centre)	Crescent Moon	Water	Silver	VAM
Manipura (Solar plexus)	Triangle (Apex down)	Fire	Red	RAM
Anahata (Heart)	Hexagon (Two interlaced triangles)	Air	Blue	YAM
Vishudda (Throat)	Oval	Ether	Violet or Indigo	HAM
Ajna (Brow)	Circle (Sun)	Cosmic Mind	Brilliant Yellow	KSHAM
Sahasrara (Crown Centre)	Lotus	Beyond all Elements	Scintillating White	OM

CHAKRA CHART II

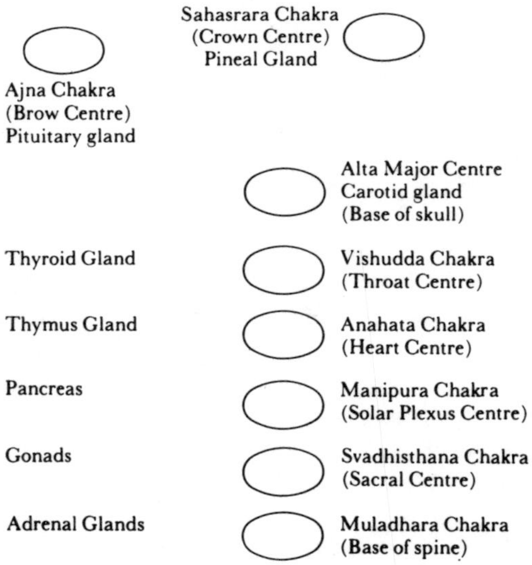

Sahasrara Chakra
(Crown Centre)
Pineal Gland

Ajna Chakra
(Brow Centre)
Pituitary gland

Alta Major Centre
Carotid gland
(Base of skull)

Thyroid Gland	Vishudda Chakra (Throat Centre)
Thymus Gland	Anahata Chakra (Heart Centre)
Pancreas	Manipura Chakra (Solar Plexus Centre)
Gonads	Svadhisthana Chakra (Sacral Centre)
Adrenal Glands	Muladhara Chakra (Base of spine)

3
A Yoga for the West

The Yoga of Synthesis

We see that spiritual growth in man moves towards the establishment of a supreme flower on the human plant – a rare orchid of great splendour, the great thousand-petalled lotus, the Sahasrara Chakra, whose radiance embraces and co-ordinates all other chakras. And yet, this flower is but one of that great inflorescences of flowers which we call the human soul. The adept not only becomes the flower, but also becomes the inflorescence. We are all part of that inflorescence. Some of the buds are not yet opened – some souls are young. The great plant of humanity may have many inflorescences, but all are part of the same tree. When someone signs a letter and puts 'Thine Own Self', you know what is meant.

But how is the flower opened so that one is able to identify oneself with one's SELF? For the Eatern Yogi, the way is through the strictest of disciplines, the sternest control of the mind, by vegetarian diet, and above all, through breathing exercises. For man in the West constantly subjected to stress, the way is not so clearly defined. We have to develop our own Yoga, adapting what methods exist to our own new environment. Our own Yoga, or Science of Union, is a Yoga of synthesis, taking what is useful and applicable from earlier Yogas.

The science of Yoga dates from remote antiquity and is revealed anew to each age. Therefore, in order to make its application practical, the techniques are adjusted to suit the evolutionary needs of mankind for that particular period of time. The four main branches of Yoga are (1) Karma Yoga, the path of work and service through right action without attachment to the results; (2) Bhakti Yoga, the path of loving devotion; (3) Jnana Yoga, the path of knowledge through self-analysis and discrimination of the real from the unreal, the Self from the not-self; (4) Hatha Yoga and its continuation, Raja Yoga, the path of bodily integration and mastery through certain psycho-physical methods and meditation. These four paths respectively correspond to the four functions of man: to sense, to feel, to think, and to will.

Experience of Wholeness

The grouping of these functions varies from one individual to another; however, everyone has two leading functions, the other two being unconscious, and consequently, undeveloped. What will be the leading function in one will be the less dominant function in another. Union, as the aim of yoga, means the experience of wholeness; it also means the unity of the four functions in the various realms of consciousness. In other words, one must learn to develop all four functions equally well and to express the appropriate function for the various situations that we encounter in daily life. What often happens is that we express our dominant function in all situations without regard for the fact that the less dominant function might be more suitable. Thus, we can take these principles and concepts from the earlier yogas and develop our own methods to meet the needs of our culture and our way of life.

This view is supported by Franklin Merrell-Wolff, a Western scientist who experienced self-realization. He writes:

> The psychical structure of the East Indian and especially of the Chinese is radically different from our own. Hence, merely to transplant methodologies which have been successful in the Orient into the Occident is a case of using the 'RIGHT METHOD WITH THE WRONG MAN'. It is only the combination of the 'right method with the right man' that works.

> This means that for the West the whole problem of devising the effective collateral aids has to be resolved in new terms. We shall have to employ the powers which we have unfolded in superior degree, rather than depend upon those which, while strongly developed in the Orient, are weak with us. Today this is a pioneering problem.[1]

The yoga that is to bring us inner radiance is not to be for the purpose of sitting in some quiet retreat like a recluse or hermit. Our yoga must be the one that will develop an integrated personality that can cope with the problems of living in this world as well as the next. Very few yogis, real yogis, who come to the West can cope with our way of life.

The promise of the coming adepts is that they will walk amongst us. If they are to live amongst us, then their Yoga will have to be adapted to such communal living. We, their younger brothers on the Path, will be required to set up various projects of world importance. We will have to organize the outer ashram for the Master to ensoul. We must provide Him with the conditions so that it is worth His while 'coming amongst us', so that His energies will not be wasted but placed in a position where they can best produce their effects for the world...a busy centralized office, a country retreat, a teaching theatre, a meditation room, a healing sanctuary, forming as it were an ashram worthy of the One Who comes. It will be the Yoga of Synthesis dedicated to serving mankind, and we ourselves must evolve it. The path to the Superconscious Experience taught by these Masters and that which Their students must follow is by MEDITATION.

Meditation

The reason we in the West do so badly with meditation is mainly because we don't know what we are trying to do in meditation. First of all, the purpose of meditation is not to gain fame, fortune, power, or psychic abilities, as many false claims and tawdry advertisements purport; neither is the

[1] *Pathways Through To Space* by Franklin Merrell-Wolff, Julian Press, 1974.

purpose of meditation to solve one's personal problems. In meditation the goal is to know our true nature, which is pure consciousness. Then, when we have contacted the totality of our being, we are in a better position to solve problems, to relate to others, and to perform our duties. It must be remembered that the purpose of meditation is threefold: (1) to produce perfect alignment of the psycho-etheric body, the emotions (astral body), and the mind (mental body); (2) to contact a higher self or consciousness which transcends the ordinary personality; and (3) to express in our daily lives, the higher energies and archetypal patterns that have been experienced on the inner planes.

And so, we need to ask ourselves, 'What are we trying to do in meditation?' The answer is that we are trying to unite our consciousness with that of a colossal Being, a great entity, a Logos, with God. When we unite our consciousness, yoke, the yogis call it, to that of a Greater Being, our mind merges into Him; we become a part of Him and we have His energies available to us. In fact, in order to understand meditation, we need to go back to two fundamental basic postulates which are most critical to the understanding of meditation.

Two Great Postulates of Ancient Wisdom

The first great postulate of Ancient Wisdom as set forth in *The Secret Doctrine* by Madame Blavatsky, is Hylozoism, the proposition that all things live. The tiniest atom is a sentinent, living entity, as is the greatest galaxy in the heavens with its immense consciousness. Everything is alive: atoms are alive, minerals are alive, gemstones are alive. More than this, the gemstones, who are masters of the mineral kingdom, radiate energies that can heal. It may seem impossible at first glance to accept the fact that what we once considered to be inanimate matter is alive, but now we have scientists who support this theory. An example of this is found in the conversations recorded by Bob Toben, a scientist, with physicists Jack Sarfatti and Fred Wolf, in the book *Space, Time and Beyond*. Although the following statements appear in this book, they could well be extracted from *The Secret Doctrine*.

> All things are interconnected...Every part of your universe is directly connected to every other part...The description of any part is inseparable from the description of the whole...You cannot move without influencing everything in your universe...You cannot even observe anything without changing the object and even yourself...It is even possible that just thinking about an object can change it and yourself...All the universe is alive...All the universe is interconnected...There is life in everything but with varying degrees of consciousness...[2]

What we are discovering, of course, is that science is not saying anything new, but is merely restating the same great Truths that were given to the world thousands of years ago in different words and symbols. Another modern, scientific view that corroborates those found in the Ancient Wisdom is given by the great Nobel prize winner, John Northrop. He indicates that it is impossible to distinguish between the animate and the inanimate, that which is living and that which is non-living, because the criterion of reproduction which is used to distinguish the living from the non-living has failed.

A typical example of this is the tobacco virus, which is nothing more than a crystal; within the cells of the tobacco plant, it is able to multiply and grow. This is also true of other viruses such as the influenza virus, which is also a crystal; they multiply and can only live within cells.

This basic postulate can be taken a step further. A family, mother, father, and children, are all living; together they are a totality called a family and have a beginning, a function, and an end; thus we can understand that a family is a living creature, a living thing. But this is also true of a tribe, a root race, a planet, a solar system, a galaxy – they are all living things having a sentient awareness, a consciousness which may be faint or vast, but a consciousness nevertheless.

The second great postulate is that all things live within the body of a greater being. For example, atoms live within molecules; molecules live within cells; cells within organs; organs within men; men within their families; families in

[2] *Space, Time and Beyond* by Bob Toben, E.P. Dutton & Co., 1975.

tribes; tribes within races; races within the body of humanity; humanity within the body of the planet; the planet within the solar system; the solar system within the body of an even greater being. These laws hold true right from the microcosm up to the macrocosm. And so, we can begin to understand that we are part of a greater being and that what is true of ourselves is also true of Him.

Earlier, we made a study of chakras within ourselves. The One in Whom we live and move and have our being, as St Paul describes it, also has seven chakras. For example, our Fifth Root Race corresponds to His throat chakra, just as the Fourth Root Race, the Atlantean, corresponds to the solar plexus chakra, and the Third Root Race, the Lemurian, corresponds to the sacral centre. He too, like ourselves, is drawing away from the sacral and solar plexus chakras and shifting his energies to the throat. The Great Occult Law of Correspondence and Analogy is well illustrated by the saying, 'As above, so below'.

One of the considerations in trying to understand something of the stupendous consciousness of these great beings in whom we live is that it gives us a key to evolve a psychological formula for ourselves, as well as an understanding of what is involved in the superconscious experience. We are talking about aligning our consciousness with that of a super being in whom we live, and when our consciousness is the same as His, we have become part of His awareness. This is what we are trying to do in meditation, and it is a stupendous thing that we are trying to achieve. It is something that ordinarily takes 500 lives on this planet, and we are trying to do it in a few short lives.

We can, therefore, understand how it is possible for a unit like a cell to share in the awareness of something greater than itself. For example, we all feel and share to some extent the awareness of our nation when it is going through a crisis. Even so, it is possible for a unit like a cell to share in the awareness of the animal in which it exists even if the experience is momentary and transient. Likewise, it is possible for a human being to have the experience of sharing in the consciousness of some stupendous being of which he is but a small part.

Analogy of the Eye

Let us consider for a moment, the following analogy in order to understand the enormity of our task. Let us suppose that a body cell, with its minute consciousness, may suddenly, in unusual circumstances, share momentarily the consciousness residing in the cells of the brain. Further, let us assume that the candidate for this initiation into this stupendous consciousness is one of the red blood cells of our own body. But first, we need to know something about the circulation of blood before we can grasp the extent of the initiation.

The red cell starts its journey from the heart laden with oxygen, and as it goes around the body, it gives out oxygen to the tissues, for that is its daily task. This takes approximately 20 seconds; then, it returns to the heart depleted of oxygen, goes through a period of rest, passes through the lungs, loads up with oxygen and returns to the heart, just as we ourselves are replenished physically in sleep. During its passage through the arteries, it experiences a certain degree of light – the ordinary light coming to it through the walls of the arteries, just as we experience a certain amount of light as we go about our work.

But because of the cell's plastic nature and malleability, one day something different happens. The cell, instead of going around in its daily task, moves up through the carotid arteries into the head region and then passes by means of very fine capillaries, to the back of the human eye to the retina. The capillaries are minute because they must not impede the light coming into the eye to the light-sensitive cones in the retina. So small are these capillaries that the red cell has to be of a very plastic or malleable nature, in order to make the passage through the *fovea centralis,* the most sensitive part of the retina where accuracy of vision is best. Herein lies a hint for ourselves to also become malleable and plastic if we wish to experience cosmic consciousness.

After much difficulty, the red cell passes along the capillary, and then for one moment, a split second, it is confronted by a light ten thousand times brighter than the light it previously knew in its daily tasks. In other words, the sort of light coming to it now through the arteries is not like the sort of sunlight that we ourselves experience in everyday life, but rather like a light that is brighter than the light of ten thousand suns. Further, at that moment of initiation into greater light, it is in a position to see what is going on outside the universe of his immediate surroundings. He may even see for a moment the direction in which the One in Whom He Lives and Moves and Has His Being is moving and is able to share in the Plan of that greater Being. Thus, we have in this analogy the sort of experience that is superconsciousness.

Part Two

The Varieties of Superconscious Experience

But these feelings are incommunicable. We have no words to express a thousand distinctions clear to the spiritual sense. If I tell of my exaltation to another who has not felt this himself, it is explicable to that person as the joy in perfect health, and he translates into lower terms what is the speech of gods to men.

A.E.: *The Candle of Vision*

Our normal waking consciousness, rational consciousness, as we call it, is but one special type of consciousness, whilst all about it, parted from it by the filmiest of screens, there lie potential forms of consciousness entirely different. No account of the universe in its totality can be final which leaves these other forms of consciousness quite disregarded – they forbid a premature closing of our accounts with reality.

William James: *The Varieties of Religious Experience*

4
Cosmic Consciousness

Superconscious Experience

Throughout recorded history there has been the testimony of noteworthy men and women who have had the spontaneous experience of illumination or cosmic consciousness. The experience has been of such an extraordinary nature that it has left its mark upon them for all time. Among those who have reported having had this awakening have been such notable contemporary figures as Pascal, Tennyson, Wordsworth, Charlotte Brontë, Walt Whitman, Nietzsche, Arthur Koestler, Merrell-Wolff, and many more.

In his book, *Cosmic Consciousness*, Dr Richard Bucke, a Canadian physician, has made an analysis of the experience of certain men and women whose achievement of a new kind of awareness places them on a different level from the rest of mankind. Notable among this compilation of reports of the superconscious experience are the accounts of such remarkable individuals as Socrates, Plato, Plotinus, Buddha, Christ, Mohammed, Ramakrishna, St Paul, Francis Bacon, Dante, William Blake, Balzac, Jacob Boehme, Swedenberg, Emerson, Thoreau, and many others. Dr Bucke points out that, although only some of mankind have succeeded in achieving the transition from self-consciousness to cosmic consciousness, all of mankind will eventually evolve to this level of awareness.

A study of the accounts reveals that regardless of the variety of religious beliefs, cultural background, geographical location, or historical period, the subjective experience of this state of awareness is identical. While the experiences described definitely transcend ordinary self-consciousness or subject-object consciousness, there are degrees and levels within this field of cosmic awareness. However, Dr Bucke fails to recognize the difference between cosmic consciousness and 'transcendental consciousness'[1] and, consequently, accords a more exalted place to Walt Whitman than to the Buddha. Nevertheless, Dr Bucke's work is valuable in understanding the nature of cosmic consciousness.

Further investigation shows that many of those who have had the superconscious experience are men of genius and are among the most talented members of the human race. It is interesting to note that if the members of this exceptional group of people were brought together at one time, they could all be accommodated in one large reception room the size of a modern drawing room. Yet the astonishing fact is that, generally speaking, these individuals have created modern civilization through their great contributions in the fields of literature, philosophy, and religion. In fact, the superconscious or mystical experience forms the basis of all great religions; it also lies at the core of such metaphyiscal systems as that expounded by Plotinus and of the philosophical systems of Socrates and Plato.

Common Factors

To those who have had the superconscious experience in various forms, it appears to have several common factors:

1. *Light* The individual is flooded with an intense light so bright that its radiance is 10,000 times brighter than the brightest sun.
2. *Omnipotence* There is a sense of power, of being able to accomplish the impossible at the moment of union.
3. *Omniscience* In addition, there is a sense of possessing infinite

[1] Transcendental Consciousness or Noumenal Consciousness is the next step in awareness beyond cosmic consciousness and is termed Nirvikalpa Samadhi by the Hindus.

wisdom and understanding at the moment of union.

4. *Timelessness* Time seems to stand still or to be slowed down.

5. *Ecstasy* Subjectively, there is an intense feeling of ecstasy or bliss which makes the orgasm of sexual union seem as nothing compared to it.

6. *Unity with All of Life* There is a sense of unity with all of life and an awareness that all other selves are 'ourself'. Also, there is the experience of the universe as a living presence, and one knows as a fact in consciousness the truth of Postulate (1) that all things live and of Postulate (2) that all things live in the body of a Greater Being.

7. *Immortality* There is a conviction of immortality which is neither a belief nor an intellectual conviction, but rather a realization of one's identity with the Greater Being; hence the fear of death vanishes.

Transformation of Personality

In all instances there is strong evidence to indicate that the experience of illumination brings about a positive change in the individual that can even be noticed by others. Outwardly, there appears to be an additional, dynamic, magnetic quality and charm that the individual did not possess before. Inwardly, there is an altered perception of the so-called external world causing a complete change in the individual's outlook on life, as well as a change in the direction of his life's goals.

In fact, in cases where the experience of cosmic awareness is not just a partial one, there is a complete transformation of the personality. This is the second birth, the rising from the tomb, that is the theme of so many myths and forms the basis of all mystery religions, including Christianity, for it represents the equivalent of the death of the old personality and the emergence of a new being. Symbolically speaking, we die on one level and are reborn on another. This is the meaning of the words of St Paul who beseeches all men:

> Awake thou that sleepest and arise from the dead,
> and Christ shall give thee light.

We are, from the point of view of an illumined being, 'dead' and do not truly 'awaken' until we have the realization of our Higher Self, which is referred to in Christian symbols as 'the Christ within'. This is the real meaning of the Resurrection and not that the tombs of the dead will open and the corpses come to life.

Essentially, to convey the positive qualities of this profound experience through the medium of words is somewhat inadequate. It is rather like trying to describe a sunrise to someone who has never seen one. In fact, many of the individuals who have experienced cosmic consciousness are quite eloquent in expressing themselves verbally, for many of them are writers of great ability. But when it comes to describing this experience, they have declared that it is almost impossible to do so. 'For thought is a bird of space that in a cage of words may indeed unfold its wings but cannot fly.'[2] However, no one who reads or hears these accounts of the superconscious experience can doubt for a moment the authenticity of their experience or fail to be convinced of the fact that those of us who have not yet been blessed with this beautiful vision 'see as through glass darkly.'[3]

[2] *The Prophet* by Kahlil Gibran, Alfred A. Knopf Publishers, 1923.
[3] St Paul's Epistle to the Corinthians, 13:1-13.

5
The Experience of Awakening

To those with occult experiences in previous lives, the awakening comes in a sudden blinding experience, as with St Paul on the road to Damascus. For him, the bursting of the inner light came as a sledgehammer blow that blinded him for three days. Plato, with his superb logic, tries to describe the sudden bursting of the inner light in his famous analogy of the cave in *The Republic*.[1] Dr Bucke also describes his own experience of cosmic consciousness in terms of light and fire. This subjective, inner fire is as real as the outer fire with which we are so familiar in our everyday life.

In the following passage from Dr Bucke's account of that eventful night, we have a classic description of the phenomenon of fire that accompanies higher states of consciousness.

> I had spent the evening in a quiet city with some friends reading and discussing poetry and philosophy. We had regaled ourselves with Wordsworth, Shelly, Browning, and especially Whitman. We parted at midnight. I had a long drive in a hansom to my lodgings. My mind traveled under the influence of the ideas, images and emotions called up by the reading and talking. I was in a state of mind of most peaceful enjoyment, not actually

[1] See *The Opening of the Third Eye* by Douglas Baker for a description of the analogy of the cave.

thinking but letting images, ideas and emotions, fleet of themselves, and spread throughout my mind. All at once, without warning of any kind, I found myself wrapped in a coloured cloud. For an instant I thought of fire, an immense conflagration somewhere close by, in that great city. The next moment I knew that the fire was within myself.[2]

Intellectual Illumination

Directly afterwards he experienced an immense exultation followed by an intellectual illumination impossible to describe. Although the illumination itself continued for only a few moments, he claims that he learned more within the few seconds during which the illumination lasted than he had learned in previous months or even years of study, and that he had learned much that no study could ever have taught. While there was no return of that experience, he never forgot what he saw and knew and never doubted the truth of what was then presented to his mind.

In the many accounts of the superconscious state, the experience is still the same, even though the interpretation of it is invariably in terms of symbols, imagery, and language common to the person having the experience. However, the symbols used to express the experience are incidental. The Christian mystic will use Christian terminology, speaking of union with Christ, with the Trinity, with God. St Paul, for example, describes it in this way: 'I live, yet not I, but Christ liveth in me.' In the Upanishads, one of India's oldest, most sacred scriptures, we find the revelations of illumined seers who declare 'Tat Twam Asi', 'Thou art That; That which is the finest essence – this whole world has that as its soul; That is Reality. That is Atman. That art thou, Svetaketu.'[3] Thus, the Hindu Yogi will describe his experience as union with the Atman, the Higher Self in man, which is the same as the Christ principle in Christianity.

On the other hand, we have the following account of a poet

[2] *Cosmic Consciousness* by Dr Richard M. Bucke, E.P. Dutton & Co., 1923.

[3] *Chandogya Upanishad*, R.E. Hume's translation.

like Tennyson who writes:

> A kind of walking trance I have frequently had, quite up from boyhood, when I have been all alone. This has often come upon me through repeating my own name to myself silently till, all at once, as it were, out of the intensity of the consciousness of individuality, the individuality itself seemed to dissolve and fade away into boundless being; and this not a confused state, but the clearest of the clearest, the surest of the surest, the weirdest of the weirdest, utterly beyond words, where death was an almost laughable impossibility, the loss of personality but the only true life.[4]

Again, the description of the experience confirms the sense of the dissolving of the boundaries of ordinary selfhood into one of 'boundless being'. It is also interesting to note that the method Tennyson used to achieve this state of awareness was the repetition of his own name, which is similar to one of the methods used in meditation practice, namely, the stilling of the mind through the repetition of a single sound.

With Edward Maitland, the superconscious experience was brought about by tracing an idea back to its origin. After reflection on an idea, related ideas presented themselves to him. These, in turn, took him back to their source, which for him was divine spirit. Interpreting this source as the superconscious realm, he says:

> I was absolutely without knowledge or expectation when I yielded to the impulse to make the attempt. I simply experimented on a faculty...being seated at my writing table the while in order to record the results as they came, and resolved to retain my hold on my outer and circumferential consciousness, no matter how far towards my inner and central consciousness I might go. For I knew not whether I should be able to regain the former if once I quitted my hold of it, or to recollect the facts of the experience. At length I achieved my object, though only by a strong effort, the tension occasioned by the endeavour to keep both extremes of the consciousness in view at once being very great.

[4] *Cosmic Consciousness* by R. Bucke, E.P. Dutton, 1922.

> Once well started on my quest, I found myself traversing a succession of spheres or belts...the impression produced being that of mounting a vast ladder stretching from the circumference towards the centre of a system, which was at once my own system, the solar system, and the universal system, the three systems being at once diverse and identical...Presently, by a supreme, and what I felt must be a final effort...I succeeded in polarising the whole of the convergent rays of consciousness into the desired focus. And at the same instant, as if through the sudden ignition of the rays thus fused into a unity, I found myself thus confronted with a glory of unspeakable whiteness and brightness, and of a lustre so intense as well-nigh to beat me back...But though feeling that I had no need to explore further, I resolved to make assurance doubly sure by piercing if I could the almost blinding lustre, and seeing what it enshrined. With a great effort I succeeded, and the glance revealed to me that which I had felt must be there...It was the dual form of the Son...the unmanifest made manifest, the unformulate formulate, the unindividuate individuate, God as the Lord, proving through His duality that God is substance as well as Force, Love as well as Will, Feminine as well as Masculine, Mother as well as Father.[5]

Again, it is interesting to note that the method of focusing the mind on an idea or symbol and tracing it back to its source or archetype as a means of reaching higher consciousness, is another well-known yogic technique documented by Evans-Wentz in *Tibetan Yoga and Secret Doctrine*.

To others, the superconscious experience occurs quite unexpectedly under the most diverse circumstances. Quite often it occurs in a moment of intense aesthetic enjoyment as it did to Warner Allen while listening to Beethoven's 'Seventh' symphony. In his book, *The Timeless Moment,* he writes:

> It flashed up lightning-wise during a performance of Beethoven's Seventh Symphony at the Queen's Hall...The swiftly flowing continuity of the music was not interrupted so that what Mr. T.S. Eliot calls, 'the intersection of the timeless moment' must have

[5] *Anne Kingsord, Her Life, Letters, Diary and Work* by Edward Maitland.

> slipped into the interval between two demi-semi-quavers...Something has happened to me – I am utterly amazed – can this be that? (That being the answer to the riddle of life) – but it is too simple – I always knew it – it is remembering an old forgotten secret – like coming home – I am not 'I', not the 'I' I thought – there is no death – peace passing understanding – yet how unworthy I –.[6]

It does not matter how varied the expression and interpretations are, the fact remains that the testimony relates an identical state of consciousness. Consider, for example, the following account of my own experiences written during the post-war years:

> Through a peculiar set of circumstances, I was introduced to a study of yoga and the Ancient Wisdom in 1950. Barely six months later, after having read the SECRET DOCTRINE by H.P. Blavatsky and the LIGHT OF THE SOUL by Alice Bailey, I suddenly had a spiritual experience one morning in May, 1951.
>
> Whilst lying in a semi-recumbent condition after a meditation, my whole body suddenly jerked into a condition of catalepsy and whilst riveted in this rigid state, a powerful force was thrust through me from head to foot. It was as if I had been catapulted into the dynamo of the universe. It resulted in the production of three principal manifestations which have been repeated again and again in various degrees of intensity ever since. I was initially aware of looking through into a new world even though fully conscious.
>
> This perception of a new dimension eventually produced in me an experience of an inner radiance, a light that made the light of our sun as nothing as compared to it. Accompanying that phenomenon was a feeling of ecstasy as I had never known before. And paralleling both new nouemena there was an accompanying sense of eternity. At first I was terrified that the experience would not return, but it did and has been mine ever since on at least four occasions every week and sometimes as many as 30 or 40.[7]

[6] *Expansion of Awareness* by Arthur Osborn, Theo. Press, 1961.
[7] *The Spiritual Diary* by Douglas Baker, March 1977.

Although many of the individuals who have had the superconscious experience have reported that it occurred once in their lifetimes, announcing itself with the suddenness of summer lightning, never to return again, there are disciplines that can be followed which will bring about the superconscious state at will and with a certain degree of regularity; one of these is through the discipline of meditation. When this is undertaken regularly over a period of time, you will begin to note some changes taking place in yourself as the growth process is quickened. You will begin to be sensitive to other dimensions of life which you will recognize as a higher state of consciousness.

Some of the varieties of subjective experiences that you will have include prophetic dreams, increased sensitivity to the environment, intuitive knowledge about things without having had access to previous information about them, awareness of causes behind effects, peak experiences, creative insights, and greater understanding of abstruse material, especially of the occult classics. All of these subjective states are descriptive of the Fourth State of consciousness, but they give you a glimpse of what lies ahead. The superconscious experience, the Fifth State,[8] is beyond all these.

[8] See *In the Steps of the Master* by Baker & Hansen for an explanation of the five states of consciousness.

Part Three

Meditation and Alchemy

Fire internal, inherent and latent;
Fire radiatory and emanative;
Fire generated, assimilated and radiated;
Fire vivifying, stimulating and destroying;
Fire transmitted, reflected and absorbed;
Fire, the basis of all life;
Fire, the essence of all existence;
Fire, the means of development, and the impulse behind all evolutionary processes;
Fire, the builder, the preserver and the constructor;
Fire, the originator, the process and the goal;
Fire, the pacifier and consumer.

The God of Fire and the fire of God interacting upon each other, till all the fires blend and blaze, and till all that exists is passed through the fire – from a solar system to an ant – and emerges as a triple perfection.

Fire then passes from the ring-pass-not as perfected essence, whether essence emerging from the human ring-pass-not, the planetary ring-pass-not or the solar.

The wheel of fire turns and all within that wheel is subject to the three-fold flame, and eventually stands perfected.

The Tibetan Master writing through
Alice Bailey, *A Treatise on Cosmic Fire*

6
Spiritual Fire, the Great Evolver

Fire of the Gods

It is important to realize that meditation,[1] when successfully taken to its culmination, is a process of energization. It is a process whereby we draw upon spiritual energy to change the whole gamut of man's visible and invisible bodies. Huge energies, which are part of a Greater Being, are literally thrust through the individual at the height of meditation. These energies are those of the Greater Being through whom we live and move and have our being. Meditation is a process whereby we go into another kingdom and steal fire from the gods. We are not normally eligible for it, but by virtue of intense discipline and by following strict instructions, we are able to go into another kingdom, whilst retaining the body of this fourth kingdom, and like Prometheus,[2] steal fire from the gods. It is this fire that energizes us, so long as we give it to mankind, like Prometheus unbound; then that fire will be available to us.

[1] We are, of course, speaking of advanced stages in meditation.
[2] Prometheus presumed to make clay men and to animate them with fire which he had stolen from heaven; this so displeased Jupiter that he punished Prometheus by commanding Mercury to bind him to Mt Caucasus, where a vulture daily preyed upon his liver, which grew in the night as much as it had been reduced during the day, so that the punishment was a prolonged torture. Hercules at last killed the vulture and set Prometheus free.

Thus, we need to understand what is involved in meditation, because in meditation we are going to be dealing with spiritual fire, the fire of the gods that Prometheus stole, the fire that we obtain from the world of soul. This fire is very real, though an inner one, and to most invisible, but then the 'fire' or 'combustion' which produces the heat of metabolism of foods is also invisible though it still consumes oxygen in what we call internal respiration. In meditation we are literally playing with fire, for the inward fire that is released has many of the same properties of the outward physical fire which is called 'fire by friction'.

The ancients noted that the only fire they ever saw was induced by lightning – lightning which came from the gods – a miraculous event. Still to this day, we do not know what fire is, and we know even less about that inward fire which H.P. Blavatsky called Fohat[3] and which stems from the centre of the sun. Science may attempt to describe fire by saying that two gases may be brought together, raising the temperature and then entering into a chemical combustion, resulting in a flame. But this simply explains the process of combustion without defining what the flame actually is. The flame is devic material, produced by fire elementals[4] and salamanders. Visible fire is the flashing into incarnation of the myriad forms of fire elementals.

However, each plane has its own kind of fire, and this is what is meant when we speak of fire by friction, solar fire, and electric fire. An example of the three fires present in all of nature is our own sun, and all three are necessary for the maintenance of form life. The description of these three fires present in the sun is given in the following tabulation:

[3] Fohat – electric fire.

[4] Devas, Elementals, Salamander – The deva evolution parallels the human evolution, while elementals are invisible entities from the deva evolution that are just beginning a course of evolutionary growth; they have been called by various names: faeries, sprites, brownies, leprechauns, etc. The Medieval Mystics gave the name of salamander to the hosts of beings associated with the element of fire.

The Central Spiritual Sun:	Electric Fire
The Heart of the Sun:	Solar Fire
The Visible Disc of the Sun:	Fire by Friction

By manipulating all three fires, man can intervene in his own spiritual evolution, becoming the alchemist who changes the dross of his own personality into the shining gold of the perfected man, the Adept, the Master of the Wisdom. Man is a god in the making, and the making involves the ever increasing capacity to channel fire.

Therefore, in order to understand the nature of spiritual fire, it is suggested that you watch how visible fire works because the inward fire can be assessed, with limitations, from an understanding of outer fire. Let us examine what fire does to water. When fire is applied to solid water, ice, it turns solid water into a liquid; when more fire is applied to liquid water, it becomes vapour; and when fire is applied to vapour, it becomes steam. Fire has transmuted, has changed, and has evolved solid gross ice into powerful, energy-releasing steam. An alchemical transmutation has occurred – alchemy has been performed with fire.

Evolution of the Root Races

Likewise, when spiritual fire is applied to man, who is 72 per cent water, he changes. Normally, when fire is applied through the long processes of evolution, man changes slowly. But when the application of the fire is accelerated by self-discipline and by meditational techniques, the fire comes through more rapidly and there occurs a subsequent rapid transmutation of the individual. Then we have occurring the appearance of those few rare individuals who seem to be ahead of their time and who are not understood by the majority of their contemporaries, but who are acclaimed and accepted by men of future races because the rest of humanity has finally arrived at a similar point in evolution through the changes wrought by the slower method of development.

Periodically, in the long course of the history of man's evolution on this planet, spiritual fire is applied systematically to the men of each of the root races as they make their appearance, and the process of change takes place slowly over aeons of time. The application of spiritual fire is, of course, determined by cosmic law and carried out by the highly evolved Beings that we referred to earlier as the inner circle of humanity, the Masters of the Wisdom. As each root race becomes eligible for the application of spiritual fire, a transmuation occurs in the life forms on this planet. The first of these major initiations occurred during the time of Lemuria when the Lords of Flame[5] from Venus applied spiritual fire to the cortex of the human brain. This gave a spurt to man's evolution as he became individualized[6] and developed the quality of abstract thought or Higher Manas which expressed itself through the sacral centre, as this was the chakra that was being integrated at that time. Today, in more spiritually evolved beings, the fire of mind expresses itself through the throat chakra, the alter ego of the sacral centre.

When fire was applied to the solid, gross, human savage of Lemuria, represented by the element earth and the corresponding astrological signs of Taurus, Virgo, and Capricorn, he changed to a being capable of abstract thought. Then more fire was applied to the man of Lemuria and solid, animal practical man became liquid, that is, astrologically speaking, he became the emotional creature of Atlantis, represented by the element of water and the corresponding astrological signs of Cancer, Scorpio, and Pisces. Under the alchemical process of spiritual fire, the man of Atlantis was learning to integrate the solar plexus chakra, which deals with the quality of emotion.

Subsequently, the fire was applied again, and the man of Atlantis changed from liquid, emotional man to the vaporous man of mentality of our Fifth Root Race who are to develop

[5] Lords of Flame – Highly evolved beings on the planet Venus which is now in its Fifth Round and therefore on a higher evolutionary spiral that the planet earth.

[6] Individualization – In esoteric parlance, it refers to the event which brought about a condition in which man gained his own soul instead of sharing a group soul.

Mortal Alchemy and the Elements

Element EARTH	Ice, Solid Water	The Savage or Materialistic Man (Lemurian: Sacral Chakra)	Capricorn Taurus Virgo
	Add Fire …		
Element WATER	Liquid Water	Emotional Man (Atlantis: Solar Plexus Chakra)	Pisces Cancer Scorpio
	Add Fire …		
Element AIR	Vapourized Water	Mental Man: Active Intelligence (Fifth Root Race: Throat Chakra)	Aquarius Gemini Libra
	Add Fire …		
Element FIRE	Steam	Spiritual Man (The new Root Race: Ajna Chakra)	Aries Leo Sagittarius

mentality to its quintessence, eventually integrating the throat chakra. The man of our present day is represented by the element of air and the corresponding astrological signs of Gemini, Libra, and Aquarius. We are at this point in time and space in our evolutionary development, and the question may well be asked as to what lies ahead.

It is said that we are now fast approaching the next major evolutionary step, and in the not-too-distant future, fire will be applied to the mental man, to ourselves, to produce a man capable of producing the power of steam and of radiating spiritual fire through his aura. Such men will be making their appearance in the Sixth root race of which the progenitors, the sixth subrace, are just beginning to incarnate. Mental man will be changed into spiritual man, and the centre that will be integrated is the Ajna Chakra, the brow centre. The element assigned to the Sixth root race is fire, represented by the astrological signs of Aries, Leo, and Sagittarius.

We see, then, that fire is the great evolver, and meditation is a process whereby we spiritually evolve through the application of inner fire to our outer nature. Fire induces change of form and growth of consciousness. As we have noted, heat, a facet of fire, changes solid ice to water, water into vapour, and vapour into steam. Likewise, through long ages man is changed from earth (solid) into fire (steam).

7
Alchemy and Transformation

Divine Alchemy

What we are speaking of here is transmutation, not of one metal to another, but transmutation at a human level. This was the basic technique of the alchemists, who noted the purifying effect of fire, as well as the way in which it melted metal or made it more malleable, so that it could be moulded into the form chosen for it by the one who wielded the fire. From this comparison was derived the concept of divine alchemy in which man on the Path subjects himself in meditation to the inner fires and becomes purified and more malleable.

This does not mean that Alchemy is a spiritual process confined only to man. It is a universal process that acts on all forms: superhuman, subhuman, animal, plant, and mineral. We live in a sea of fire and to the eye of an adept, that fire is seen. Pause for a moment and visualize every atom that exists; each emits the light of its fire as electrons in the atom move outwards from orbit to orbit. Visualize every cell that is and the fires they emit as the combustion of metabolism provides it with energy. Consider then also that beneath every living form there is a fire raging, and you will have a concept of what is meant by that 'sea of fire'. And so the statement, 'My God is an all-consuming fire,' has real meaning for those who meditate.

In his book, *Pathways Through to Space*, Franklin Merrell-Wolff, a contemporary Western scientist, makes an outstanding contribution to mystic literature in his account of the spiritual transformation he experienced through the alchemical process of spiritual fire. The following is a description of his personal experience.

> A Fire descends and consumes the personal man. For a time, short or long, this Fire continues. The personal man is the fuel, and the fuel, in greater or less measure, does suffer. But fire does not destroy; it simply transforms. This fact can be realized by an analysis of what takes place through the action of ordinary fire. If a log is burning, the fuel is principally, if not wholly, in the form of carbohydrates, and the fire transforms these into carbon dioxide and water vapour. There remains a small amount of ashes, the persistently earthly portion of the log. The carbohydrate in the log was a fixed form, partaking, for a time, of the earthly solidity of the mineral associates in the log. But as the carbohydrates become carbon dioxide and water vapour, they take on new form in the freer world of the air. So too, does the Fire which descends and consumes the personal man but Transforms him. Only the ash of the personal nature is left behind, while the rest, the best of the personality, is taken up to be conscious in airy spaces. The ultimate state is one of a far, far greater Joy...He who identifies himself with the fuel predominantly suffers much and keenly, but if, on the other hand, he unites himself with the Fire, all is changed. The Flame of the Fire is a dance of Joy.[1]

Each human soul is a unit of energy, a transmitting station for solar fire, a radiation that stems from the heart of the sun, which has the effect of evolving all living things that come into contact with it, of energizing them, and of using them to express the qualities of Love-Wisdom. In the physical vehicle of man, the tissue which makes up the vagus or tenth cranial nerve[2] and its ramifications, is the most receptive to this solar

[1] *Pathways Through to Space* by Franklin Merrell-Wolff, Julian Press, 1974

[2] See *In the Steps of the Master* by Baker & Hansen, and *Esoteric Healing* (Part II) by Douglas Baker for a detailed study of the vagus nerve.

energy. It is, thus, esoterically speaking, said to be 'sacred' in the sense that the minor lives or elementals which make it up are evolving hierarchies, whilst those which build the rest of the physical body, are on the involutional path. The seven chakras, of which five are in manifestation in human form at any one time, are also transmitters of this solar fire, and through the endocrine system, are closely linked to the vagus nerve.

This solar energy, a manifestation of spiritual fire, reflects outwardly from the soul to the other vehicles, registering itself in different ways as it pours through the aura:

1. As illumination and clairvoyance through the brow chakra.
2. As sacrifice through the throat chakra by healing and helping others.
3. As compassion for all living things through the heart chakra.
4. As intuition through the solar plexus chakra.
5. As the 'will to be' through the sacral chakra.

Kundalini Fire

With respect to the subject of spiritual fire, it is important to clarify the matter of kundalini fire. At a cosmic level, we witness before our normal vision, the visible disc of the sun which demonstrates Fire by Friction in the Macrocosm. Fire by friction is also found in the very centre of the earth and has been called kundalini fire. This fire constitutes the energy of the first life wave to pour out from the Logos, or third aspect of the Trinity, and is a manifestation from the previous solar system. This same fire is also found in man, the microcosm, and produces the Fire of kundalini in him also. It is this fire which constitutes the essence of the internal fires of the body cells as well as that of the root chakra at the base of the spine called Muladhara. The kundalini energy or force from the earth is also absorbed by the root chakra and acts upon man, giving the dense physical body health and functional vigour. It must be remembered that kundalini has a number of different levels of expression which have nothing to do with the arousal of the serpent fire at all. The Fire exists in layers, and it is only when the innermost core of the Fire is activated that kundalini is truly aroused.

Many so-called authorities of yoga rate kundalini fire as the highest possible manifestation of spirit; it is nothing of the sort. Kundalini, a negatively charged energy, is aroused by the influx of positively charged energy, Electric Fire, which is found in the central spiritual sun. When Electric Fire, Fohat, pours through Sahasrara, the crown chakra, kundalini hears the call of her mate and rises from her cave in the base of the spine, to meet Him. In the same way, it can be truthfully said that the release of the energy of nuclear fission represents arousal of planetary kundalini. For the first time in the history of the planet, its kundalini is being released consciously and under the control of a higher centre. That higher chakra or force centre in the planet, which we call the human kingdom, is stimulating that centre at the base of the spine of the Planetary Logos (the mineral kingdom) in the production of atomic energy. As a result, we have the flow of planetary kundalini to higher force centres or chakras, which is Yoga on a planetary scale.

The Fire of kundalini, the fire of matter, is aroused as a final step in man's spiritual development. There is much misapprehension about the raising of kundalini, but let us assure you, it is most difficult to raise. Only when it progresses geometrically up all three spinal tracts, ida, pingala, and sushumna, with simultaneous action and uniform vibration, is true kundalini fire aroused, and it can only be done by the Higher Self. Then, when all three fires merge and blend in man, he emerges as a perfected Being, and the powers latent within him are fully expressed.

Thus, man is slowly changed by solar fire through the long process of earthly evolution and persistent rebirth. But man can be changed rapidly by the Divine Alchemy of meditation, a process whereby Solar Fire is consciously brought to bear on the personality and on the mental, emotional, and physical bodies of which it is composed. Man is prepared for entry into the Fifth Kingdom and moves from mortality to immortality, from transience to permanence.

Part Four

Group Meditation

No man is an Iland intire of itselfe;
every man is a piece of the Continent; a
part of the maine; if a Clod bee washed away
by the Sea, Europe is the lesse, as well as if
a Promontorie were, as well as if a Manner of
thy friends or of thine owne were; any man's
death diminishes me, because I am involved
in Mankinde: And therefore never send to
know for whom the bell tolls; it tolls for thee.

John Donne

8
The Mission of the New Age

The Age of Aquarius

Today, mankind stands on the threshold of a new age as the solar system enters the zodiacal sign of Aquarius. The influences of the Age of Pisces, which reigned for the last two thousand years, are dying out as the Age of Aquarius sweeps into manifestation, bringing with it emphasis on group relationships, group service, and group meditation. Consequently, the changes in the types of meditation change too. For one thing, meditation is becoming less personal. Previously, it was practised by the chela in some secluded retreat or ashram or by the monk in his piscean monastery. Now, however, one of the main qualities emerging through the sign of Aquarius is for group expression, that is, for groups that are capable of acting, serving, studying, and meditating together, as a single entity. This brings to mind Postulates 1 and 2 mentioned earlier, that all things live and have their existence in the body of a Greater Being. The 'body of a Greater Being' includes families, businesses, nations, races, humanity, and so on, right up to the Planetary Logos and Solar Logos.[1]

The Age of Aquarius has a special esoteric mission which is the preparation of what will become immense groups for initiation in the Age of Capricorn that follows Aquarius.

[1] Planetary Logos, Solar Logos – The Beings that use a planet or a solar system to express themselves through.

Initiation is the process whereby spiritual Fire from Sirius is applied to the head centres of the candidate and is channelled by the Planetary Logos himself, and then stepped down by two attendant Masters of the Wisdom before it reaches the head centres of the individual. This phenomenon short circuits the slow unfoldment of man through the natural process of 'endless' rebirth. Concurrently, there is an extension of awareness and a change in level of being, as well as an increase in the capacity to carry the life force. It must be emphasized that no mortal can initiate you. There are five major initiations on this planet. The Fifth Initiation brings adeptship, admission to the extra-systemic Lodge from which the Sirian[2] force originated, and release from the Wheel of Rebirth.

However, Initiation for many an earnest and sincere disciple is frequently impossible because of some serious defect in karma, dharma, or personality of the individual. Perhaps, through an educational mishap, there is inability to study or even to meditate as a single individual, but this may be compensated for by working within a group. Part of the members may be able to conduct study group meetings on a particular book or subject which could be encompassed by that person unable to study on his own. Similarly, if only three people in a group meditation are reaching the Buddhic plane, then the whole of the group is rewarded karmically and otherwise. This is carried to its fulmination with eligibility of every group member for the Initiation of the group as a whole. Such stimulating results of the Initiation would, normally, not have been available to some of the individuals struggling on their own.

Man's New Responsibilities

As man undergoes expansions of consciousness through the process of alchemy, increasing responsibility is placed upon him for his actions. Millions of years ago, the man of Lemuria crossed from the animal kingdom into the human kingdom

[2] Sirian Force – the evolutionary force from the Star Sirius.

through the event called Individualization as extra-systemic Fire was applied to the cortex of his brain. (See Part Three, *Meditation and Alchemy*). This does not mean to imply that man descended from animal forms, i.e., from the anthropoid apes, as suggested by the Darwinian theory of evolution. According to the theory presented by ancient, authoritative sources, the form that man inhabited was animal-like and 'mindless' until that Fire was applied.[3]

Parallelling this great extension of consciousness, man became responsible for his actions; animals are not responsible for their actions; their cruelty, their sexual appetites, etc. This is the symbolic meaning of the biblical story of Adam and Eve in the Garden of Eden. By eating the fruit of the tree of knowledge offered to them by the serpent, Adam and Eve become self-conscious and are thus separated from the animals, who do not possess this awareness. Since they are no longer part of a Group Soul, they must pay the price for individualized consciousness; because they are now responsible for their acts, they are exiled from the Garden of Eden.

However, it is not surprising to find that the serpent that was responsible for their exile can also lead them back to the Garden and to oneness on a higher turn of the spiral. In the Egyptian Mysteries this is symbolized by the image of a serpent with a tail in its mouth, representing infinity, the unending continuity of life. In Hindu Yoga the phenomenon of kundalini, which is associated with enlightenment, is also represented by a serpent which is lying asleep at the base of the spine. The awakening of the serpent represents the higher awakening in man as he once again experiences unity with all of life and becomes group conscious.

Today man is even more responsible, for man's responsibilities increase with his awareness. Because of improved communications through the mass media, vast

[3] *Anthropogeny: The Esoteric History of Man's Origin* by Douglas Baker and *The Secret Doctrine* by H.P. Blavatsky for a description of the two evolutions.

numbers of mankind are made more aware of planetary problems. This requires us to become more and more involved in helping to solve the problems of mankind, for we are our brother's keeper, and not only are we our brother's keeper, but also the guardians and protectors of the lower kingdoms. As part of a group, an individual assumes greater responsibilities as he learns to shoulder the burdens of the group, as well as be part of its projects in its service to mankind. It is this sharing in responsibility that necessitates a new look at meditation techniques.

Group Meditation

Group meditation is becoming increasingly popular, and many who would not normally meditate on their own will now do so in groups. It is important to remember that, in order to form a group, any three people can come together for this purpose. Two people do not and cannot form a group. There is such instability between two points (of consciousness) that with access to increased energy, oscillation and instability would soon set in. Generally, this expresses itself as domination of one point over the other at some level, so that the latter becomes a satellite. A partnership between two, therefore, does not imply the qualities that emerge and are associated with a group relationship. A group is more than the sum of its parts, and when thoroughly integrated, that is, when there is true mergence of the individual's identity and desires with those of the group, the individual partakes of the energies and consciousness of the whole in which he 'lives and moves and has his being'.

However, the truth of the matter is that of all meditation procedures at this time, group meditation has the poorest performance. But whenever three people in a group are aligned with each other and are truly meditating, then miracles can be wrought. The effects are far more potently felt than the sum total of individuals meditating on their own. Group meditation by highly spiritual beings with a background of experience in personal meditation can accomplish unbelievable results. For example, much of the evolutionary spurt of the present epoch is the result of effective meditation by groups of adepts.

Contemporary group meditation usually takes the form of an assembly of people in which one individual 'leads' the meditation by spoken words and highly directed thoughts. Then, at the highest moment, those present are asked to remain silent for a few moments and to 'hold themselves in the Light', before the meditation is drawn to a close. If only three participants have indeed reached the heights of meditation and stayed there in unison, then the meditation has been successful. But the usual result is that most people, not having learned correct meditation procedures, find that their minds are wandering and that they are fidgeting uncomfortably during the entire meditation period. Inwardly, they wonder whether things are really happening in the way in which the meditation leader is describing it. Of course, there are some who experience a feeling of well-being and upliftment because they have raised their thoughts to a higher level. Although this is desirable, it is not meditation. Group meditation will need a lot more hard work before its effects become powerfully felt and before some of the lesser known facts behind the whole exercise become better known.

Yoga on a Planetary Scale

Let us examine these facts a little more closely in order to understand what should be transpiring in group meditation. In Part One we saw how Man on the Path must build a link or antakarana to his Soul. This rainbow bridge creates a channel for the entry of higher energies into his aura. The Planetary Logos is, on His own plane, endeavouring to do the same. He seeks to build the antakarana between earth and her alter ego, which is the planet Venus, to create a bridge between the planetary mental energies of Active Intelligence (Ray Three) of the Earth, and the higher mental planes, which are the fields of expression for Those Who inhabit Venus. Success of this project, an act of yoga on a planetary scale, would bring transformation of the Earth with the same sort of rapidity of transformation that occurs in a man who makes contact with his soul in meditation.

At the present stage of planetary endeavour, this bridgehead with the Earth's alter ego needs establishing at the level of the etheric. Just as our own physical bodies are built into an etheric matrix, so too, is the physical body of the Earth. Through an inheritance from the last solar system, the etheric body of our planet in its entirety is constructed out of patterns of etheric squares, and during our present solar system, the endeavour is to transform these square lattices into triangular structures. The planetary antakarana would be the first structure to conform to this triangular pattern, and, thereafter the whole etheric body of the planet would follow suit with a transformation of all Kingdoms of nature.

9
Techniques for Group Meditation

World Triangles

What each of us can do with comparative ease, is to build triangular networks of light on the surface of the planet and beyond. The method used is to make a contact with two like-minded friends and to form a triangle with them. At least once a day, preferably at times that are coincident, link up with them, holding them in your thoughts and circulating the energies of Goodwill. As you see these energies flowing between you, visualize a triangle of light linking each of you and a vortex of energy rising from the interplay. At the same time, sound the Great Invocation (see later) and follow this with the sounding of the Sacred Word, OM, knowing that you are helping to build the planetary etheric body into a network of triangles as part of the divine plan. Later, you may establish more triangles with members of your family and other friends.

The degree of success of your triangles will depend on the depth of feeling put into their creation and maintenance. The element of Will applied to their construction and their energization is also just as important. The reason is that the whole keynote of the Earth is to be changed. If the keynote of Mars is Regenerative Energy, often Blind and Destructive, and that of Venus is Abstract Thought and Harmony, what is the note of the Earth? At this time, it is not a note that bears thinking about; at best it must surely be no more than Pain and Separativeness. We do know what the note should be: it should be Goodwill and by that we mean World Goodwill. We often say, 'Peace on Earth, Goodwill to all Men,' little knowing how close these phrases are to esoteric truths. Unhappily, they are characteristic only at certain festive seasons where the note is blunted by other emotions and lax forms of expression.

However, it is far more important to know what the note of the future is to be, for therein lies the endeavour of the disciple and the candidate for initiation. The note that will drive forward the antakarana of the Earth to its alter ego is The Will to Good. Hence, the reason for expressing both deep feeling and will in the establishment and maintenance of the Triangles you build. These triangles are essentially invocative and will form the basis of future religions and the evocative sciences that go with them.

We have seen that shapes are accumulators of energy and triangles are no exception.[1] The creation of a Triangle, depending on its intensity, invites within it energies from the planes where symbols are all-important, i.e., the plane of Higher Manas, the residence of the Lords of Flame, those selfsame Beings who brought the Fire of individualization to the cortex of man's brain on this planet, nineteen million years ago. It is in this second field of meditation that man's new responsibilities demand his active participation in planetary affairs at the level of his soul.

Planetary and Full Moon Meditation

Groups and individuals using this technique of planetary Triangles meditation can obtain a very high efficiency in a comparatively short time with far-reaching effects. This is because man co-operates with the forces of nature while meditating and sacrifices himself as a channel for cosmic forces. At times, beneficial cosmic forces are so tremendous, that even if every human on the planet were acting as individual channels, they could not cope with the pressure of extra systemic forces being directed towards our earthly evolution.

[1] See *The Jewel in the Lotus* (Section Three) by Douglas Baker.

The Great Invocation is used at the period of the full moon by many individuals the world over at full moon meditation meetings to re-direct the excessive energy being showered on earth at that time. Members join together when the moon is full, holding a common theme in their minds as they join in planetary meditation. As we mentioned earlier, the meditation theme for our planet at this time is 'Goodwill to All Men', and as the Aquarian Age swings into full manifestation, the theme will change to 'The Will to Good'.

The reason why the full moon cycle has so much importance is that the earth is receiving the combined light of the sun and the moon at that time. Consequently, the increased light flooding the earth corresponds to a point whereby the planet earth has a moment of opportunity, spiritually speaking, and we all can join in on it. The Planetary Logos has his moments of meditation too, and the most spiritual time for Him is at the time of the Full Moon. The occult significance of the waxing and waning of the moon is that it corresponds to the in-breathing and out-breathing of the planet itself.

Those who are familiar with the practice of yoga know that the act of respiration lends power to any thought held in the mind. There is a great difference between breathing in as you think and breathing out as you think. If we wish to construct or strengthen a thought, we breathe in, and that will give the thought outline, for the intake of prana strengthens the thought. When the breath is held prior to exhalation, the thought consolidates. When we breathe out, the thoughtform can be sent out from us towards its target. At the moment of complete exhalation, the thoughtform may be destroyed or held latent.

When the moon is waxing, it corresponds to the inbreathing of the planet, and new concepts can be strengthened and built up. For the three-day period when the moon is full, such concepts can be consolidated, and then during the waning of the moon, the visualized patterns can be projected to their destination as blueprints for some earthly venture or to reinforce at subtle levels, a project that has already begun.

This offers everyone who would sacrifice his time at the full moon the opportunity of sharing in the construction of ideals or in the planned destruction of established projects on a planetary scale.

Tremendous Stress

At the precise moment of the full moon, the earth is placed under tremendous stress, as it hangs suspended exactly between the sun and the moon, all three forming a straight line. Man on the Path is also sensitive to the stress, spiritual and otherwise imposed on the planet at the time of the Full Moon. Emotionally polarized individuals find the full moon period particularly distressful, and psychic instability shows itself in the unrest noted in asylums at that time. On the other hand, mentally polarized individuals find the time of the full moon a particularly productive one, especially if a great deal of mental work is to be done. The tremendous cosmic energies and higher vibrations flooding the earth at that time can give us a momentary glimpse of what the application of solar fire to the head centres would be like; and that is the reason why stern disciplines are imposed on the candidate, so that he can withstand the fire when it is brought down in meditation or by some other means.

You can assist in planetary meditation at the time of the Full Moon, either by joining others at Full Moon Meditation meetings,[2] or alone in the silence of your meditation room. Mark on your calendar the Full Moon periods 12 months ahead. For the three days over the full moon period, focus your attention on gathering spiritual forces on the planet, remembering that the 'spiritually aware' are the reservoirs for

[2] For further information regarding Full Moon Meditation procedures and World Triangles and the World Goodwill Movement, contact Lucis Trust, 866 United Nations Plaza, Suite 566-7, N.Y. N.Y. 10017. You should register your own triangles with this organization, where they can be integrated with the triangles formed by thousands of others on the planet, whom the Master D.K. referred to as 'The New Group of World Servers'.

those forces. Say the Great Invocation, visualizing your chakras above the diaphragm being filled with the energies described by each verse.

From the point of Light .... Ajna Chakra
From the point of Love .... Heart Chakra
From the centre where .... Head Chakra
From the centre which .... Throat Chakra

For the twelve-hour period when the moon is fullest, stand in the light using the Great Invocation, almost as in Japa.[3] Then, as the moon wanes, direct the light to those in need, to the dark places on our planet, where there is much pain and suffering. Choose a different target for your spiritual energies in each cycle: hospitals, prisons, the aged, the sick, the poor, etc.

So far we have been discussing group meditation and in the next section we will consider individual meditation. Having a basic foundation in this type of meditation will assist greatly in group meditation.

The Great Invocation is the property of no one, and is not exclusive to any particular religion, sect, or group. It is a world prayer translated into over fifty languages and dialects; it is widely used at the time of the Full Moon.

The Great Invocation

From the point of Light within the Mind of God
Let light stream forth into the minds of men.
Let light descend on Earth.

From the point of love within the Heart of God
Let love stream forth into the hearts of men.
May Christ return to Earth.

From the centre where the Will of God is known
Let purpose guide the little wills of men –
The purpose which the Masters know and serve.

[3] Japa – continuous repetition of a mantra.

From the centre which we call the race of men
Let the plan of Love and Light work out.
And may it seal the door where evil dwells.
Let Light and Love and Power restore the Plan on Earth.

Part Five

Individual Meditation

How long will you tread the circling tracks of mind
Around your little self and petty things?
A seer, a strong creator is within,
This transient earthly being, if he wills,
Can fit his act to a transcendent scheme.

Aurobindo

10
The Eight Limbs of Yoga

Yoga Sutras of Patanjali

Foremost among the teachings of Yoga are those of the sage, Patanjali, whose Yoga Sutras form the authoritative treatise for the practise of Raja Yoga, the branch of Yoga which deals with the science of meditation. In these sutras are found the rules and methods which bring the mind under control, stabilize the emotions, and develop the thread of consciousness which leads to knowledge of our true nature and to the superconscious experience. It should be noted that, in the East, the development of practices that lead to realization of the Self were motivated by man's attempt to liberate himself from pain and suffering. Hence, this main concern gave rise to the major religious philosophical systems of the East. The Yoga Sutras of Patanjali is one of the systems developed to release man from suffering and to lead him to Self-Realization.

The progress outlined in the eight steps or 'limbs' of the Sutras was obligatory for all spiritual aspirants. At later periods, spiritual teachers elaborated this programme so that the special temperaments of different seekers could be developed. As a result, a number of specialized types of Yoga were evolved, namely, Hatha Yoga, the science of physical postures; Karma Yoga, the path of right action; Bhakti Yoga, the path of devotion; Mantra Yoga, the science of sound vibration; Jnana Yoga, the path of knowledge. However, Raja Yoga is considered to be the aim of all the other Yogas, as it results in the transcendental experience. For clarification, it should be noted that the word 'Yoga', refers both to the path and to the goal. Thus, when one speaks of practising Yoga, what is meant is that the student is following the disciplines for achieving the goal of Yoga, union.

Patanjali, a sage who lived about 200 B.C., was not the originator of this system of Yoga. Rather, what he did was to restate Yoga philosophy for the man of his day. He condensed this material into a highly selective form known as a 'sutra'. A sutra[1] is a short statement which binds together an underlying continuity of ideas in outline form. There are a total of 196 sutras, and although they occupy less than ten pages of large print, they set forth an elaborate outline of psychology and philosophy. Since Patanjali knew that his followers needed no convincing, he did not concern himself with persuading or special pleading. Therefore, what he gave was a comprehensive theory that could be verified by personal experience.

Personality Integration

Patanjali and his followers were fully aware of all that is referred to in modern terms as the collective unconscious and the collective superconscious. Likewise, they had their own methods for dealing with complexes, fixations, and the problems related to personality integration. In recent years there has been an increasing number of studies made of the similarities between Eastern and Western methods of psychotherapy. One of the most striking comparisons between Eastern and Western approaches to growth and enlightenment is found in the work of the renowned Swiss psychologist, Professor Carl Jung. His four phases of analysis bear a remarkable resemblance to the work of Patanjali and the whole age-long tradition of the search for enlightenment.

As a matter of fact, it has now been realized that both the Eastern Guru and the Western psychotherapist perform the same function in their relationship to disciple and patient; for

[1] Sutra means thread in Sanskrit.

Yoga, like the Jewish Kabala and Western Analytical Psychology, is a system for inner growth, personality integration, and ultimately Self-Realization. That Jung is in full agreement with the Eastern approach is apparent in the following comment:

> To experience and realize this Self is the ultimate aim of Indian Yoga, and in considering the psychology of the Self, we would do well to have recourse to the treasures of Indian wisdom. In India, as with us, the experience of the Self has nothing to do with intellectualism; it is a vital happening which brings about a fundamental transformation of personality. I have called the process that leads to this experience the 'process of individuation'.[2]

The term 'meditation' is used in such a variety of ways to designate a diversity of practices that differ so widely from one another that it is necessary to explain what is meant by meditation in Raja Yoga practice. The way in which it is used in Yoga is in a formal and disciplined sense that excludes intellectual activity; as such it differs from reflection on a subject. Raja Yoga meditation includes two processes: making the mind introspective or one-pointed, and bringing to total cessation the thought waves in the mind.

In the second sutra, Patanjali gives his famous definition of Yoga: 'Yoga is the inhibition of the modifications of the Mind.' Through ethical development and meditative techniques, the thoughts are stilled and the mind is made serene, ultimately leading to Samadhi, the superconscious experience. Interestingly, the ability to still the thought waves in the mind can only be achieved after we have dealt with the contents of the lower unconscious. Like Dante,[3] we must first grapple with the Dweller on the Threshold, purify our threefold nature, and integrate our personalities before it is possible

[2] *The Practice of Psycotherapy*, Vol. 16, The Collected Works of C.J. Jung, Pantheon, 1954.

[3] For a further discussion of this subject, see *In the Steps of the Masters* by Baker and Hansen.

to still the thought waves in the mind and experience this union that is called Yoga.

This demands sacrifice, self-discipline, and sustained effort. It is interesting to note that the Sanskrit word for effort is 'tapas', meaning that which generates energy or heat. When the term, 'tapas', is applied to human conduct it means the practice of conserving energy and directing it towards the goal of Yoga. Obviously, in order to do this, we must exercise self-discipline regarding our moral and ethical conduct; we must learn to control our physical appetites and passions. It is for this reason that the moral and ethical injunctions are placed first on the list of procedures to be followed to achieve the superconscious experience.

Astanga Yoga

Patanjali's system of Raja Yoga is often referred to as 'Astanga Yoga' because he outlines eight key practices or limbs to transcend the mind and achieve Samadhi. Although these stages follow each other in natural sequence, implying a stepwise development, in actual practice several of the stages or limbs may be engaged in almost simultaneously. For example, the last three steps, which are Dharana, Dhyana, and Samadhi, translated as fixation, sustained concentration, and absorption, constitute a single process in advanced stages of meditation. This triple process is designated by one word in Sanskrit, Samyama, and presupposes an advanced degree of control in concentration. When Samyama is performed on any object, including the solar system, the true nature and direct knowledge of that object can be accurately known.

The eight limbs of Yoga are enumerated below:

1. Yama (Abstentions)

a. Harmlessness
b. Truthfulness
c. Non-Stealing
d. Continence
e. Non-Covetousness

2. Niyama (Observances)
   a. Cleanliness
   b. Contentment
   c. Fiery Aspiration
   d. Self-Study
   e. Self-Surrender to the Higher Self

3. Asana (seated posture)

4. Pranayama (control of prana)

5. Pratyahara (withdrawal of the senses)

6. Dharana (concentration or fixation)

7. Dyhana (sustained concentration)

8. Samadhi (superconscious experience)

Naturally, variations and discrepancies occur in the translation of the Sanskrit words into English. This is because of the difficulty of conveying an abstruse philosophical concept into a language that has no equivalent meaning for the same word, with the result that sometimes distortions and loss of original meanings occur; hence the need for lengthy commentaries on each of the sutras.

The first two limbs or steps, which are called, Yamas (abstentions), and Niyamas (observances), comprise a total of ten injunctions that formulate the moral and ethnic guidelines for the aspirant. The five Yamas (the 'shalt not's') prohibit violence, lying, stealing, sensuality, and greed. Of course, it is important to understand that the virtues prescribed have a much wider scope and deeper significance than what appears on the surface. Judging from ordinary standards, the injunctions against killing, lying, stealing, etc., do not represent a high degree of morality. However, what is meant is that the virtues have to be practised at a higher degree of perfection and must be interpreted at a subtler level. For example, the injunction against violence is understood not only from its gross meaning of not killing or injuring another, but also from the more subtle meaning of not wanting to kill or injure. Ultimately, the cultivation of this virtue results in freeing the individual from thoughts or images of violence.

Likewise, the injunction against lying extends to the subtler interpretation of deception. We may be clever in thinking that we are deceiving others about our character, but oblivious to the fact that we are really only deceiving ourselves. We would do well to heed the advice of the immortal bard in cultivating the virtue of truthfulness.

To thine own self be true
And it shall follow as the night the day
Thou canst not be false to any man.[4]

The injunction against stealing has reference to abstention on the emotional and mental planes. Thus, the aspirant does not claim such emotional benefits as love and favour, dislike or hatred; on the mental level, he does not claim a reputation not warranted or the assumption of another's duty, favour or popularity.

Sensuality and Greed

Another trap is sensuality and greed; the endless search for pleasure, not only with regard to sexual indulgence, but on all levels must be carefully moderated, because the search for pleasure only leads to a further search for pleasure and uses up a great deal of the life force. On the other hand, greed, the acquisition of more and more material possessions, which is never satiated, creates more and more attachments. In the end these pursuits only lead to pain and suffering and to deeper involvement in material things. Eventually, man learns to understand that his endless pursuit of pleasure in the external world is really a search for the Self.

The five Niyamas (observances) are cleanliness, contentment, fiery aspiration, self-study, and self-surrender; these are qualities that are to be cultivated. Again, we must go beyond the obvious interpretation to a deeper meaning of these observances. Cleanliness does not stop at the physical level, but goes beyond it into the emotional and mental realms. The passage of spiritual Fire into the aura will focus on any impurity, whether it is physical, mental, emotional, or

[4] *Hamlet* by John Richardson through William Shakespeare.

etheric, and will be detained there. Mental and emotional contamination such as fear, worry, anguish, etc., constitute pollutions of the subtle vehicles and must be dealt with. The aspirant must also deal with the mental contaminations produced by his environment, social life, work, etc.

Contentment does not mean satisfaction, but rather an acceptance and recognition of where one is on the path and of one's present assets. This assessment and acceptance produces a calm state of mind for pursuing the goal of enlightenment. Although the aspirant has developed a sense of acceptance with his present level of progress, at the same time, he continues to strive towards his goal. The quality needed for this is fiery aspiration, which refers to the sustained effort to continue onward up the mountain towards the ideal envisioned. The student continues to practice the daily disciplines faithfully in spite of the fact that there may be little or no indication of any advancement being made, and regardless of the feelings of discouragement and despair that creep in after the initial burst of enthusiasm has worn off. Only when this quality has been developed and proved is anyone permitted to become the disciple of some Master.

Occult Classics

Briefly, self-study in this context means the study of the occult classics, such as *The Secret Doctrine* or *The Treatise on Cosmic Fire,* and such spiritual scriptures as *The Bhagavad Gita* or *The Yoga Sutras*; it also includes other instructive material that leads to self-knowledge and union with the Self. As such, the study should also include an understanding of symbols, as this will help to develop one's sense of the subjective realities. Carried a step further, it will be found that all forms, including the three-fold personality, are symbols that veil or hide a divine idea or truth. When this is understood, the disciple seeks to contact the divine essence hidden by the forms in all kingdoms of nature.

Self-surrender to the Higher Self, or to the Master within, may be described as constituting the attitude of the lower three-fold personality to the service of the Master within or the

Christ within the heart. The attitude to be cultivated is to perform our service in the world without thought of success or failure. We sometimes forget that the reason we are in physical manifestation is for the evolution of consciousness, and not to serve our own personal ends.

These virtues are to be cultivated in order to eliminate completely all mental and emotional disturbances that characterize the life of an ordinary human being. Furthermore, the Yamas and Niyamas not only serve as a moral and ethical code of conduct, but also as a means of attaining non-attachment, conserving the life force, and sustaining one-pointedness of concentration. The conserved energy is used to advantage in practising the techniques of the following six steps, while the practice of non-attachment implies freedom from attraction and repulsion of sense objects, thus overcoming the disturbing influence of the emotions in trying to still the thought waves in the mind.

11
Preliminary Measures for Meditation

The remaining six limbs of the meditation procedure may be synthesized into four main stages in order to simplify the steps and to have a plan of the procedure constantly on hand. They are:

a. Seating oneself
b. Withdrawal of the senses
c. Concentration
d. Meditation (sustained concentration)

It is important to realize that necessary preliminary measures should be observed to ensure that conditions ideal for meditation prevail before the discipline is attempted. The first of these is seating oneself, and this means having a place to meditate, 'a room of one's own', a sanctuary wherein you may retire and commune with your soul uninterrupted by family or friends. Since this room should be a place in which the vibrations are maintained at a high level, it should not be used for other activities or by other people or by your pets. Neither should you enter your sanctuary when you are having emotional upheavals, because this destroys the high vibrations created in meditation and brings in those of a lower order.

The daily use of this room for meditation purposes only will raise the vibrations to such a high spiritual level that when you enter, the effect is felt immediately, and part of the struggle to raise the vibrations during the time of meditation is eliminated. Then when you sit down to meditate, proper alignment of the vehicles is achieved in a matter of seconds, thereby saving a little more of the precious time you have available for meditation.

Having a room of one's own does not imply that you need to build a new wing onto the house or that the room should be used exclusively for that purpose. If the space available to you is limited, you may want to screen off a corner of your bedroom or of the basement to use as your 'meditation room', but that tiny section of the room must be your own and no one else's. Furthermore, in order to assist in the creation and maintenance of high thoughts, provide your meditation room with freshly cut flowers, if possible, or with potted plants that will help to ionize the air.

Ionization is greatly enhanced if the potted plants are mounted in a box through which an electric current is passing. By placing the potted plant above a generator of high tension direct voltage, with a small alternatinge current superimposed, we can turn plants into ionizers in our homes for therapeutic benefits as well, as this is especially beneficial to asthmatics. Ideally, the air in the meditation room should be negatively charged, since negative ions assist, through breathing, to concentrate the electrical energies of the body in the head region during meditation. This is the sort of atmosphere found in the centre of the pyramid and which is also produced by rivulets and fountains.

Another item that is helpful is to have a stained glass window in the room with both your sun sign and the rising sign. The use of colour in your meditation room is extremely important; therefore, if you are unable to provide yourself with a stained glass window, you may avail yourself of a substitute by using dharmaseals. These are colourful transparencies of mandalas and yantras[1] which can easily be

[1] Mandala – a symbolic representation of a universal concept which includes colourful geometric designs along with Eastern deities. A yantra is similar to a mandala, but is basically a simpler structure, comprising geometric designs only. Both are used widely in Tibet in meditation practice.

applied to any surface, and especially to windows, so that when the light shines through them, they give the appearance of a stained glass window.

Both the use of colour and sound in your meditation room attracts deva hosts, the same minute beings who assist in the building of mental substances in visualization. The devas see sound and hear colour; therefore, by taking crystals from old chandeliers and hanging them to tinkle in the open window, you will attract these thought elementals. If the crystals are prismatic and hang in places where the sun can strike them, they will flash the colour and the qualities of the Seven Rays[2] through the room.

The Masters

In addition, include valid pictures of the Masters in your meditation room. These should not be displayed in a place where they would arouse the curiosity and comments of others. The portraits will instil reverence and inspiration and may also be used as a focal point in the meditation practice. Remember, also, that the Masters are present in their portraits and in their works; therefore, this is where your library of classical teachings of the Ancient Wisdom should be kept. The Masters have either written the books or have inspired them through Their first-hand knowledge of the tortured path which men must take to reach the heights. Most prominent among the authors of such works are H.P. Blavatsky, Alice A. Bailey, Annie Besant, Gurdjieff, Ouspensky, C.W. Leadbeater, Rudolph Steiner, Swedenborg, Paracelsus, Plato, and Eliphas Lévi.

The use of music as a preliminary to meditation is highly recommendable. It often acts as a device for centring because it helps to align the vehicles. Ideally, music should be used whose tune and melody cannot be distinguished; Gregorian chants are helpful for those whose astral body is always at a flashpoint. There are also some Zen Buddhist chants and

[2] For an explanation of the Seven Rays see *The Seven Rays: Key to the Mysteries* by Douglas Baker.

Hindu mantras that have an extremely potent effect on the vehicles and are excellent for attunement to higher dimensions. Whether or not you understand the meaning of the Sanskrit words is not important; what is important is the effect of the sound on your vehicles.

Indian classical music, especially the ragas, are designed to effect one's level of consciousness through sound. There are, for example, pre-dawn, dawn, noon, and evening ragas which are played at those specific times of the day and which are designed to work on your consciousness in a certain way. Certain forms of Western classical music also have this effect. It is said, for example, that Bach was describing the universe at the causal plane through sound; hence listening to Bach would also have the effect of raising consciousness to another level prior to meditation. In the East there is a science based on the effects of sound vibration on the human being which is called Mantra Yoga.

Not only does music and mantra help to prepare the individual prior to meditation, but the reading of inspirational material beforehand also helps to prepare the way. The reading of the occult classics for half an hour before sitting down to meditate has the same effect as listening to music or chanting mantras; it helps to key you in immediately to the Ashram from which the material first originated. Then when you seat yourself, you will find that your thoughts are already tuned in to another dimension. The same thing happens when you read material written by individuals who have had the superconscious experience or even when you read their biographies of their struggle to reach the heights. Whether you select music or reading material or both, you will find that aligning the vehicles and focusing the mind occurs with greater ease and rapidity.

Incense

The use of incense in a room has both a physiological effect and a psychic effect. Physiologically, it results in vasoconstriction of the blood vessels in the nasal septum, thereby unclogging stuffed nasal passages and allowing for freer passage of air and, most important, of prana which is vital in meditation practice. The psychic effect of incense is that of raising the vibrations of the room because the presence of astral entities of the lowest order find it difficult to manifest in the presence of high vibrations and of incense. Not only does incense help to eliminate unwanted odours, but also to get rid of lower level thoughtforms and negative emotions. Generally speaking, it has an uplifting effect and makes it easier to pass into deeper levels of awareness. Be sure to purchase a high quality incense; otherwise, you will find the scent a distraction rather than an aid to your meditation. It is recommended that a joss stick of incense be used which lasts as long as the meditation session.

Since there is a wide range of incense to choose from, select a scent that enhances the quality of your meditation. If, for example, these effects create or add to aspiration, or reverence, or recall of previous spiritual experiences, then that particular scent is recommendable. Later, when the Ray of the Soul is known, the corresponding incense to that Ray may be used to help establish alignment and *rapport* with the Soul. For example, sandalwood incense is on the First Ray of will and power and affects the chakras on the spine, for all will chakras are on the spine. If you use jasmine, which is a Second Ray incense, it affects the Love Ray chakras lying just in front of the spine, namely the heart chakra, solar plexus chakra, and the brow chakra. Cinnamon is Fifth Ray, while frankincense and myrrh is Seventh Ray, and rosewood is Sixth Ray, expressing the qualities of devotion and idealism. Remember that Rays 1, 3, 5, and 7 are designated as Will Rays, whereas Rays 2, 4, and 6 are the Love Rays.

When you understand the Ray Psychology, you will be able to apply this knowledge in choosing an appropriate incense to help develop or change some of the qualities in yourself that are needed. This does not mean that incense alone will bring about the needed changes, but it is one of the methods that can be used to stimulate the chakras that need activation in order to express a quality that is lacking. Thus, if your ray analysis indicates a strong preponderance of Will Rays, then the required balance is in the direction of expressing more of the qualities of Love-Wisdom. If, on the other hand, the analysis shows a strong tendency toward Love Rays with little or no will being expressed, then the need is to balance these energies with those of Will and Power. Remember that we are striving to become whole, and so every effort in that direction brings us a step closer to union with the Higher Self.

Candles

The room you are using for meditation should be in semi-darkness, preferably with no electric lights in use, or with just a dim one if it is at night. It is suggested that you have a lighted candle that burns along with your incense while you are meditating. The lighted candle is a symbol of the Divine Flame, the Monad, that is really yourself; it is also symbolic of the spiritual fire that is brought down into your aura during the height of meditation. The candle may also serve as a focal point of concentration in the practice of Tratakam, the candle gaze. Be sure to light your candle and incense when you seat yourself.

Length of Meditation

Another important consideration is the length of time to spend in meditation and the best time of day to meditate. At first, you must treat all gently; to begin with, a half-hour of meditation in the morning is sufficient. Later, you may add a half-hour at midday and a half-hour in the evening, so that there are a total of three meditation periods a day. As you near initiation, these periods can be altered and increased because at this time, periods of withdrawal are most important.

Clothing

If it is possible, have a special robe for meditation that is worn for that purpose only. If you know the Ray of your Soul, then you may choose a colour related to it. If you do not know the Soul's Ray, select a colour that appeals to you, and that will most likely be the correct one for you. Also of importance is to use the same blanket, rug, pillow, or chair to sit on for meditation. Whatever you use to sit on should only be used by you and only for activities related to meditation. In other words, you would not bring the blanket you use for meditation to a picnic or allow your pet to sleep on it.

Again, it is important to understand that the whole purpose of using the same clothing and seat for meditation is that you are building thoughtforms in mental matter and creating higher vibrations during the meditation period which are being reinforced each time you sit down for meditation. These articles have your vibrations on them, and to use these articles for other purposes weakens the thoughtforms and vibrations you are creating at the time of meditation and destroys some of the precious work you have striven so hard to achieve.

Food

Also related to the disciplines grouped under 'seating oneself' is that of eating. For at least two hours prior to meditation, no food should be eaten. The reason for this is that some of the prana, cosmic energy, is being used to digest the food you have just eaten instead of being channelled to the head region, where it is needed at the time of meditation. A certain amount of energy is required each day to maintain ordinary awareness, but for higher states of consciousness, greater quantities of energy are needed than that required for our normal state of consciousness. Without a sufficient amount of prana, it is difficult to focus the mind in meditation and to register the higher awareness on the physical brain consciousness. This is why it is important not to meditate when you are tired or sleepy. At those times, just learn to sit in silence instead of trying to pursue your meditation practice.

12
The Spiritual Diary

One of the most important of all the disciplines, major and minor, grouped under 'seating oneself', is the keeping of a spiritual diary. The open diary, placed in front of the stained glass window, should constitute the focal point of the room. From its sum total of entries, the Master is able to assess at any time of the day or night where the student is on the Path, what his needs are, and the fields in which his service can be most effective. The daily entries, sometimes even hourly, are minor replicas of 'seating oneself'.

The diary should be a notebook with blank pages rather than a day-to-day diary with the days printed on it. Days may go by without a single entry because nothing has happened; this can be somewhat disconcerting if you have pages and pages of labelled days where you have nothing to write down. Therefore, chose a plain note-book and write in the date as you make your entries. There may be times when you will have as many as ten entries in one night because the spirit forces are flowing through you.

At the outset it should be made clear that the diary does not involve the daily entry of the day's events and has no relation to the happenings which concern the personality. As a matter of fact the Master is not concerned with your personality problems. His main concern is with spiritual matters and only with those personality issues that are directly or indirectly concerned with your spiritual endeavours. Hence, you enter into your spiritual diary whatever represents your highest efforts. The diary should include entries under the following three headings:

1. All subjective experiences.
2. A record of the occult classics you are studying and the problems that arise from them, i.e., questions that need answering.
3. How you have been of service to your fellowmen in the last 24 hours.

The Master Wants to Know

Include under the heading of subjective experiences, anything of a subjective nature that occurs in moments of quiet and in meditations, such as symbols, spiritual perception, intuitive knowledge, creative insights, mental telepathy, and impressions that are not registered by the five senses. If you had a sensation of warmth, or colour, or light, or energy flooding you, put it down; the Master wants to know. At the same time, learn to discriminate the real from the unreal, i.e., what may be aberrations or lower psychic experiences from what is directly the expression of the inner reality. Pay due attention to symbols and record them without trying to interpret them at first.

Also include a record of your dreams under this heading, and extract symbols from them, compiling a list of these and their meanings at the back of the diary. Later, you will find that when you are attached to a certain Ashram, it has symbols which mean certain things. Usually, the initial contacts which a Master makes with a disciple are through visual impressions. That is why your waking dreams are so important, because that is the time that the Master or an Initiate from the Ashram is trying to contact you. Therefore, these dreams should be recorded and pondered over and related to events that have recently occurred or which take place later.

Secondly, record your efforts to study the occult classics. You should have three works under your attention at any one time. For example, heavy works like *The Secret Doctrine,* or *The Treatise on Cosmic Fire,* should be approached when you are alone; for instructional purposes works such as *The Bhagavad*

Gita, Patanjali's Sutras,[1] *A Treatise on White Magic,* or *The Jewel in the Lotus* are of great value. Write down the title of the book you are studying, together with parts of these books that you don't understand, and you will find that you will get the answers from the Masters either through dreams, or visions, or in meditation, or in a quiet moment. List your questions in your diary and leave the diary open at these questions when you meditate or go to sleep, and the Masters will advise you because They either wrote the books or They use them. Furthermore, when you focus your attention on works vibrating to Their wavelength, a strong interplay occurs between your Ajna Centre and the Ajna Centre of the Ashram. For the Westerner, the Ashram of immediate concern is linked in some way to that of the Master K.H. or the Master M.

Finally, under the third heading, entries related to the services you are rendering to mankind should be recorded. What sacrifices are you making for humanity in helping to raise their consciousness? How are you helping your fellowmen along the Path? How are you spreading Goodwill? What esoteric venture do you support financially or actively? How do you spread the Wisdom? To what projects do you send your energies at the time of the Full Moon? Only you can give answers to these questions and the appropriate place for them is in the spiritual diary.

Emergence of the Third Eye

Note that each of these disciplines energizes a chakra; meditation energizes the crown chakra; study of the occult classics energizes the brow chakra; and service to mankind energizes the Alta Major chakra. The simultaneous arousal of all three of these head centres results in the emergence of the Third Eye.[2] In other words, the Third Eye emerges from the

[1] For an excellent commentary on the Yoga Sutras, read *Light of the Soul* by Alice A. Bailey, Lucis Trust, N.Y.

[2] See *The Opening of the Third Eye* by Douglas Baker, Aquarian Press, 1977.

vortex of energy created through the interplay of the three head centres when they are aroused.

Each entry into the spiritual diary is a reminder of your apprenticeship to your Higher Self. On the Path of Discipleship the relationship of the disciple with his own Soul becomes of prime importance. To review your entries at any time, constitutes a minor revelation in itself. Such a review gives the same sensation as one experiences watching a flower opening. You begin to note cycles and rhythms of growing awareness down through the years, the causes of obstruction to spiritual growth, as well as the stimuli.

Your diary becomes your confessional and your mentor. The keeping of it promotes orderliness and absolute honesty in dealing with matters spiritual from the masses of impressions streaming into an awareness primed by meditation, down to each single motive behind the daily activities. No other discipline can bring to your notice more quickly the foibles of your thoughts, words, and deeds, your backslidings into glamour, the foolishness of self-blame and guilt, and the extent of your limitations and potential, than the keeping of a spiritual diary.

As an act of dedication, you should perform a simple and effective discipline each day. Copy (in longhand) into your spiritual diary, four or five lines from either *The Voice of the Silence*, by H.P. Blavatsky, or *At the Feet of the Master*, by J. Krishnamurti. These books are written in small sections or paragraphs, which lend themselves to such entries. When the entry is made, spend as much time as you can pondering over the meaning of the words, and then make entries in a different coloured ink, under the lines, giving your interpretation.

This discipline will serve three purposes. Firstly, it will encourage introspection and pupation; secondly, it will serve to encourage you and gird you to greater effort, and thirdly, it will spiritualize the diary. This is effective when the whole text is contained in the diary. It means that the Ashram that put out the teaching of the particular occult classic used, is *en rapport* with it, especially when it is written in personal handwriting in the diary.

The totality of the diary in any one day gives off a symbol. From a glance at the diary, the Masters know immediately where you are in time and space on the Path, what your needs are, and what your difficulties are. Through the diary, the Masters are able to reach you at any time of the day, and they will help you. Therefore, the purpose of seating oneself becomes evident: to create the proper atmosphere conducive to meditation and to bring in higher energies. The disciple sounds his note in meditation, in the 'room of one's own', and sets up a vibration of a similar wavelength in the appropriate Ashram. This *rapport* can lead to an interplay and exchange of energies which is the basis of soul contact in meditation.

13
Posture and Control of Prana

Asana (Seated Posture)
The word Asana in Sanskrit means posture. In Raja Yoga, this means where the meditator sits and how he sits. Although Patanjali does not elaborate on this limb, he is, of course, referring to one of the various folded-leg positions in which the meditator will be able to maintain a comfortable steady posture. In Hatha Yoga, however, Asana refers to a number of postures, other than the folded leg positions. In fact, many who do not know anything about Yoga confuse it with these physical postures. It must be understood that the purpose of Hatha Yoga is considered by some authorities to be a preparation for, and to form part of, the Raja Yoga system.

The goal of Hatha Yoga, which consists of postures, along with its elaborate system of pranayama, is to strengthen the body and nervous system and to purify the nadis in the etheric vehicle for the entry of spiritual Fire during Raja Yoga practice, which is meditation. In other words, it prepares both the physical and etheric vehicles to endure the downflow of Solar Fire into the aura, as well as the increased flow of Fire into the organs themselves. Clearly , the physical brain and the nervous system are the weakest links in withstanding the downflow of spiritual Fire, as those who have had the experience can verify.

The results of Hatha Yoga practice produce endurance, vitality, and health in the physical body, and it is precisely the 'health' aspect of Hatha Yoga that has attracted the Westerner to this discipline. There is no doubt that many have benefited from the health viewpoint, but health is simply a by-product of Hatha and not its primary goal. There are, of course, other objectives of Hatha Yoga practice which are neither known nor understood by the Westerner; these are primarily to unite the two currents generated in respiration, known as the prana vayu and apana vayu, and to direct prana into sushumna nadi, the central spinal tube in the etheric body. Because the two prana vayus manifest in a positive-negative situation, it is believed that the restlessness of the mind is caused by their opposition. Therefore, by uniting the two currents, the mind becomes quiet and steady. Likewise, when prana is directed from the right and left nadis, which also manifest as a polarity, into the central canal, the breath is automatically suspended and the flow of thought waves is halted. However, let us emphasize again that spiritual development is not dependent on these asanas or on Hatha Yoga practice.

Folded Leg Postures

The folded leg postures include Padmasana, lotus posture, Siddhasana, half lotus, and Sukhasana, cross-legged position; these positions provide both steadiness and comfort. However, it is not necessary to sit in a cross-legged position, and you may seat yourself in an easy chair if it is more comfortable for you. In either case, you must be seated firmly so that you do not fall forward in meditation. There is, however, one advantage in being seated on the floor in a cross-legged position and that is because the currents of the earth centre of your aura, represented by the feet, are in contact with the magnetic currents of the Muladhara Chakra. This enables certain magnetic currents in the etheric body to be redirected and for latent magnetic reserves to be available for greater activity.

If you do seat yourself on the floor, be sure to use a folded blanket or cusion to sit on, making sure that the ankles have sufficient padding under them. In addition to this, you may need a support for the lower back, as this part of the body tires easily and brings you out of the alpha state quickly if any discomfort is felt there during meditation. The body must be placed in such a comfortable position that it does not cause any disturbance during the time of meditation. There is nothing so disconcerting as having your back ache or your ankle fall asleep while you are trying to withdraw the senses and focus the mind on your object of meditation. Of primary importance, however, whether you seat yourself in an easy chair or whether you seat yourself on the floor, is that your spine must remain upright or erect in order to allow for the free passage of energies through the body. Note that you do not sit with a straight spine, for if you did your spine would be deformed. An upright spine has natural curves. It is also possible to meditate in a horizontal position providing, of course, you remain awake. Nevertheless, you finally arrive at a point in meditation where you are hardly aware that you have a body at all, and this is why so much emphasis is placed on seating oneself; many never get beyond this point at all and give the whole thing up.

Since the practice of the frontal gaze, turning the eyes upwards and inwards is used later in succeeding stages of meditation, it is recommended that you practice eye exercises

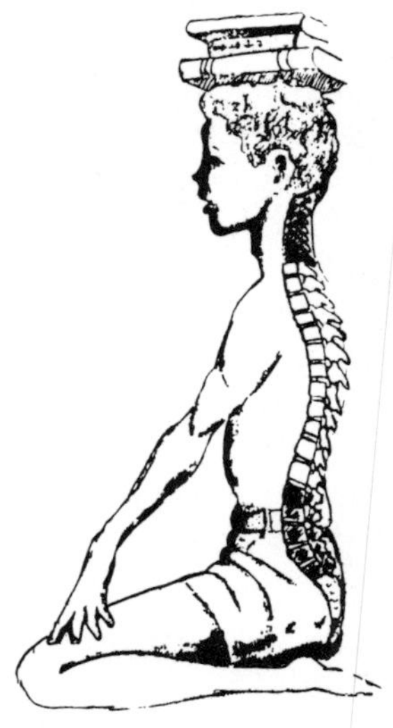

4. An Upright Spine Has Natural Curves.

twice daily in order to strengthen the six eye muscles and to prevent painful stiffness. Essentially, the eyes should be rotated three times from left to right, up and down, diagonally, and circled clockwise and anticlockwise. Without this preliminary preparation, pain and discomfort result from the attempt to sustain the frontal gaze during meditation practice.

Pranayama (Control of Prana)

The next limb in Patanjali's system is Pranayama, which is the control of prana through breath control and visualization. Pranayama[1] is not, as many think, the regulation of the breath, but rather the control of prana through the conscious manipulation of the breath. Prana, cosmic energy, is necessary for the vitalization and functioning of all vehicles of consciousness, physical or subtle, and that is why pranayama plays such an important part in the practice of yoga.

Although Patanjali does not stress the practice of pranayama, he does recommend the regulation of the breath through rhythmic breathing and a slowing down of the breathing cycle through inhalation, retention, and exhalation of the breath for a certain fixed number of counts. Most of us are not aware of the fact that there is a relationship between mind and breath. It has been found, for example, that erratic, irregular breathing produces restlessness in the mind, and conversely, a restless mind, as well as negative emotions, produce erratic, irregular breathing. A rhythmic, even flow of breath has a quieting effect on the mind, while states of joy and calmness produce a regular even breath. Hence, by slowing down the breathing rate and by breathing rhythmically, there is a slowing down of the thought process, which is a prerequisite in meditation. It has also been found that in moments of deep concentration, there is almost a

[1] Pranayama – The nature of Pranayama is indicated by the two words Prana (cosmic energy, or vital force) and Ayama (restraint). It means the regulation of Prana. Prana is the vital force, not the breath.

suspension of breath, along with a cessation of thought.

Breathing Technique

While Pranayam is utilized to a minimum in other yogas, in Hatha Yoga, it becomes an entire science. Essentially, the breathing technique involves the intentional suspension of breath at the end of a measured inhalation or at the end of a measured exhalation. Technically, the retention of breath, either after inhalation or after exhalation, is called Kumbhaka, and is the essential element of real Pranayama. There are thus three main elements involved in Pranayama: they are inhalation, (Puraka), retention of breath, (Kumbhaka), and exhalation (Rechaka). The period of Kumbhaka is gradually increased over a period of time, and its practice affects the flow of Pranic currents in a very marked way, enabling the practitioner to eventually direct these currents consciously. Many commentators caution that no one should practice advanced Pranayama without the constant supervision of an experienced teacher.

Deep breathing, or diaphragmatic breathing, has nothing to do with Pranayama, and may be practised as an exercise for promoting health. Its beneficial effects depend chiefly upon the increased intake of oxygen and the greater influx of Prana into the body, but it does not affect the Pranic currents. On the other hand, alternate nostril breathing affects the Pranic currents to a certain extent, but its main purpose is to purify the nadis, especially Ida and Pingala, removing the congestion from the channels in which Prana normally flows. It must be remembered that the vehicle of Prana is not the dense, physical body, but the etheric vehicle called Pranamaya Kosha. Of course, when we breathe normally, the Pranic currents follow their natural course. Alternate nostril breathing, without the retention cycle, is a preparation for Pranayama and has a tranquillizing effect on the mind. This breathing exercise may be practised effectively as a preliminary to meditation.

When sufficient control of Prana has been developed, either through the practice of Pranayama or by having reached a certain stage of spiritual development, then breathing ceases of its own accord while the meditator is deeply absorbed in concentration. In a state of Samadhi, the breathing ceases altogether for a considerable interval of time. This kind of suspension is not dangerous because it can only take place when an individual is sufficiently developed and is able to support it.

Of the cessation of breath during his superconscious experience, Yogananda writes:

> My body became immovably rooted; breath was drawn out of my lungs as if by some huge magnet. Soul and mind instantly lost their physical bondage and streamed out like a fluid piercing light from every pore. The flesh was as though dead, yet in my intense awareness I knew that never before had I been fully alive. My sense of identity was no longer confined to a body, but embraced the circumbient atoms.

He continues with a long, vivid description of his literally breathtaking experience, and then concludes:

> Suddenly the breath returned to my lungs. With a disappointment almost unbearable, I realized that my infinite immensity was lost. Once more I was limited to the humiliating cage of a body, not easily accommodative to the Spirit. Like a prodigal child, I had run away from my macrocosmic home and had imprisoned myself in a narrow microcosm.[2]

Another important breathing exercise that should be practised as a preliminary to meditation is the bellows breath. It also acts as a cleansing agent and relaxant for the nerves, but its chief importance lies in the fact that its use brings electrical charges into the head region, which is important in the later stages of meditation.

This breathing exercise is the technique that must be used

[2] *Autobiography of a Yogi* by Yogananda, Self Realization Fellowship, 1957.

at the highest point of meditation when concentration has been reached upon a visualized point within and you are, as it were, on a razor's edge. At this moment, as you stand on the inner and outer consciousness, there is no time to search for a suitable breath. You have to practice it frequently beforehand, so that at the right moment you automatically start doing the appropriate breathing exercise. It should be easily introduced into the procedure in such a way that the precious concentration of the equally precious visualized pattern is not in any way disturbed. The act of starting the bellows breath should be virtually a reflex to that decisive moment of intense concentration.

Technique for the Bellows Breath

After seating yourself and lighting your candle and incense, you may begin the next stage by practising the bellows breath (Bastrika Pranayama). This comprises short, quick forceful movements that are performed with the abdomen while the breath is drawn quickly and sharply through the nose, causing the nostrils to flare; simultaneously, a snoring sound is heard as the breathing is executed. The chest moves as little as

5. Technique for the Bellows Breath

possible, and the movements are performed rhythmically. Start by performing a short, quick exhalation through the nose while simultaneously contracting the abdomen. Without pause, execute a quick and forceful inhalation through the nose while simultaneously expanding the abdomen. Continue without a pause to the next exhalation with accompanying contraction of the abdomen and so on, until ten rounds are performed while facing forward.

Then the head should be turned sharply to the left with a repetition of the same procedure of ten rounds. The head is turned back to the forward position and the process is repeated; again, turn the head sharply to the right and repeat the whole process for another ten rounds. This makes a total of forty rounds. Whilst a degree of alkalosis is recommendable and is obtainable through over-breathing, when done excessively, it can lead to a 'blackout'. Therefore, this practice should be slowly developed with adequate care that no 'blackouts' occur through the manner described. Upon completion of the last cycle, take a complete breath, hold to capacity, and exhale. In advanced practice, the three Bandhas, or locks, are applied during the retention cycle: chin lock, stomach lock, and anal lock. When you have completed the cycle of bellows breath and the complete breath, sit quietly

6. Alternative Nostril Breathing.

for a few moments, breathing normally, and become aware of the indescribable peaceful state of your entire being.

Alternate Nostril Breath

With the completion of the above breathing cycles, you may begin the practice of alternative nostril breathing. Remember to sit comfortably, keeping the spine erect.

With the index and middle fingers folded, place your right thumb on your right nostril, and your ring finger and little fingers on your left nostril. Then exhale through both nostrils. Close your right nostril with your right thumb and inhale slowly through your left nostril. Keep the right nostril closed and close the left nostril also, so that both nostrils are closed.

Hold the breath as long as you comfortably can, then release the pressure on the right nostril, exhaling through it, while holding the left nostril closed. When the exhalation is completed, immediately begin the next inhalation through the right nostril. (This is the same nostril through which you have just exhaled.) Then close the right nostril so that once again both nostrils are closed, holding the breath as long as it is comfortable, then exhale through the left nostril holding the right one closed, and you are again ready to inhale through the left nostril.

Now you have returned to the original starting point. Each time you return to this starting point, you have completed one round of alternate nostril breathing. Five rounds of breathing are sufficient for your practice, with a rhythmic count for each cycle.

Ideally, the rhythm to work towards is a ratio of 1:4:2. Thus, you would inhale 4, hold 16, and exhale 8. Since this is an advanced rhythm, in the beginning it is wise to start with a ratio of 1:2:2, inhaling 4 counts, holding 8, and exhaling 8. Again, the three locks may be applied during the retention cycle; and in advanced Pranayama, the number of breaths and rounds is gradually increased. At the conclusion of this breathing cycle, you may sit quietly focusing your attention at the Ajna Chakra and visualizing that centre as a brilliant sun.

There are a number of visualization practices that can be

engaged in while performing alternate nostril breathing. One of these is to inhale Prana in the form of a white light, bringing it down the left side of the spine as you inhale through the left nostril. During the retention cycle, the attention is focused on the Muladhara Chakra. With the exhalation, visualize the white light travelling up the Sushumna Nadi to the crown chakra. While inhaling through the right nostril, Prana is visualized descending on the right side of the spine. Again the attention is held at the base of the spine during the retention cycle; with the exhalation, Prana, in the form of a white light is brought up the central channel to the crown centre.

The Full Breath

Another useful exercise that helps to energize the aura and the chakra is the complete breath with visualization. This is simply to perform diaphragmatic breathing with breath retention to the ratio of 1:2:1 or 1:2:2 to start with, and later increasing it to 1:4:2. Thus, you may begin by inhaling 8 counts, holding 16, and exhaling 8; or by inhaling 8, holding 16, and exhaling 16. If you use the ratio of 1:4:2, begin by inhaling 4, holding 16, and exhaling 8. As you inhale, imagine a sphere of brilliant white light about 6 inches above your head. Maintain this visualization during the breath retention cycle; then with the exhalation, see a shaft of brilliant white light moving downwards from the sphere, entering the crown chakra, descending on down through your body, enveloping and flooding the whole body with light. As you inhale once again, see the brilliant white sphere above your head and repeat the process five times, making a total of five rounds in all.

When proficiency is established in this visualization, you may want to add the following visualization as a variation. Once again visualize a sphere of white light above your head, but this time, as the shaft of light enters the crown chakra, it develops into a sphere of white light at the brow chakra, then, as a shaft of light moves down from there, it blossoms into another sphere of white light at the throat chakra, and so on, until you have visualized a sphere of light at each of the chakras; this sequence is performed five times. The energization of the aura and chakras by the use of this method is very powerful, and you will experience a tingling sensation throughout the body upon completion of this exercise.

Mantra

At this point you will find it extremely beneficial to sound the OM seven times by vibrating the O in the chest and the M in your head. Equally powerful, is the sounding of the OM in each of the chakras. Simply feel each chakra, starting at the base of the spine and travel upward to the crown chakra, sounding the OM in each centre as you go up the spine. If there are other mantras that you know, such as the Tibetan mantra *Om Mane Padme Hum* (Oh, the Jewel in the Lotus), you may use them at this time. When you stop chanting, sit quietly for a few moments and feel the vibrations.

Even if you should stop the meditation process at this point and go no further in your practice for that day because of pressing needs or lack of time, you will find that you are experiencing an elevation and upliftment of your entire being, a state of euphoria reminiscent of the Fourth State. This feeling will remain with you throughout your entire day and will enhance the quality of whatever you do, and will radiate from you to those you meet.

An interesting variation of the Tibetan Mantra *Om Mane Padme Hum* can be used in conjunction with the visualization of colour. A simplified form of this mantra has only three sounds: OM AH HUM. With the in-breath visualize the colour of blue while mentally sounding the syllable HUM. During the breath retention cycle (Khumbaka), visualize the colour red and mentally sound AH; with the exhalation, visualize the colour white and mentally or audibly sound the OM. The colours should be visualized in the Ajna Chakra. There is no question that colour and sound can effect us profoundly, and by using the right combinations of both, it is possible to affect our inner development, thereby bringing about a more rapid unfoldment.

Along with the sounding of the mantra OM AH HUM, the

significance of the three syllables is to be held in the mind. On the cosmic scale, the in-breathing and the syllable HUM corresponds to the 'Night of Bhrama' when the worlds lie in an unmanifest state and represent an indrawing process; the retention cycle and the syllable AH correspond to the building of the thoughtform; while the outbreath and the AUM or OM represent the 'Day of Bhrama' and the reappearance or manifestation of the created worlds.[3]

[3] In Hindu philosophy, the 'Day of Bhrama' and 'Night of Bhrama' correspond to two enormously long periods of time of equal duration called a Kalpa, which totals 4,320,000,000 years.

14
Withdrawal of the Senses

Pratyahara, the withdrawal of the mind from sense objects, is really the withdrawal of the mind into itself so that there is a complete severance of connection with the external stimuli of the outside world. The senses are really the outposts of the lower mind in the external world, which keep us anchored there in our waking state. The energies from the higher planes that pour into us are dissipated and diverted by the many diversions in the outer world demanding our attention and which prevent us from gently withdrawing from the world. Therefore, it is a very difficult stage for the Westerner because in Pratyahara, the abstraction from the world is so complete that the sense organs cease to function and the mind has no object of attraction in the external world.

You are well aware of what happens when you are absorbed in an interesting book and someone comes into the room and speaks to you; but you neither see nor hear anything because your attention is turned away from those sensations. Although a high degree of abstraction is attained in such cases, the abstraction is involuntary and there is something in the external world on which the mind is concentrated.

Brainwashing

If we examine what occurs in political brainwashing, we will have a clearer understanding of what occurs in Pratyahara, withdrawal of the senses. When political victims are brainwashed, they are placed in a plain cell with nothing to distract them. The light is either on all the time or there is complete darkness all the time, so that they are unable to tell what day of the week it is or the time of day. There are no newspapers or reading material of any kind; nothing to divert the mind. At this point, because the mind is not anchored to anything in this world, it becomes unstable, but at the same time malleable and receptive to political indoctrination. Likewise, in Pratyahara, when the mind is unable to anchor itself to the outside world, it eventually becomes receptive to something interior that will attract it.

The monks in the Christian monasteries were in exactly the same situation. In the monastic orders, the monk was placed in a bare cell with nothing to do except pray and to count his beads. Although he had a certain regime to follow each day, there was no access to the outside world and he became receptive to the teachings of the Mother Church. It is the same with you; you must make yourself receptive to the teachings of your own Soul.

Through the process of Pratyahara, withdrawal of the senses, you too are brainwashing yourself, but it is a voluntary act. You are introducing yourself to the teachings of the human Soul, not to our teachings, not to anyone else's teachings, but to what your Soul has to say to you. Your mind has to become receptive because the 'Voice of the Silence' is not heard in waking consciousness. Only when you shut down the senses can you hear the voice that has no sound, and only then will you experience the light that casts no shadows, for you will be in touch with your own Soul.

The brainwashing technique we have been describing is similar to the experimental work done by Dr John Lilly with the sensory deprivation tank. He undertook these experiments on himself for the U.S. government in order to find out what would happen to astronauts when they are freed of sensory input. The scientists hypothesized that outside stimulation was necessary in order to keep the brain awake and that the lack of sensory input would result in sleep.

In his book, *The Centre of the Cyclone,* Dr John Lilly describes how he immersed himself in a tank of water of the same temperature of his body. All sound and light were cut off and all stimulating clothing was removed. The physical sensation in the tank was as if one were floating in space free of gravity. Dr Lilly discovered that far from going to sleep, he had extraordinary experiences in which his mind left his body and went to other dimensions. Later he found that the phenomenon he was experiencing was described in various literatures and the states he was experiencing resembled those attained by other techniques.

Describing his experiences in the tank, Lilly writes:

> In these experiences, I came across what one might call 'supraself', and 'supraspecies metaprogrammers', which seemed to me to be outside myself, not imbedded in me. Using other languages, other terminologies, one could call these celestial gurus, or divine teachers or guardians. I also got into spaces where the energies and the forces were so vast that there was no humanly conceivable way of transmitting these experiences in words in a book.
>
> ...I went through dreamlike states, trancelike states, mystical states. In all of these states, I was totally intact, centred, and there. At no time did I lose conscious awareness of the facts of the experiment. Some part of me always knew that I was suspended in water in a tank in the dark and in the silence.
>
> I went through experiences in which other people apparently joined me in this dark silent environment. I could actually see them, feel them, and hear them. At other times, I went through dreamlike sequences, waking dreams as they are now called, in which I watched what was happening. At other times I apparently tuned in on networks of communication that are normally below our levels of awareness, networks of civilizations way beyond ours...[1]

If there is any danger in meditation, it is now, in the early processes which lead to true meditation, because with sensory input withdrawn, the mind becomes unsure of itself, a little unstable. This is why you need to follow the teachings of esoteric instruction so carefully to be safe. We hear a great

[1] *The Centre of the Cyclone* by Dr John Lilly, Bantam Books, 1973.

deal of nonsense about arousing kundalini; none of this will arouse kundalini. But what may happen is that you could have a difficult period in which you reorient the mind.

Withdrawing the Senses

There are many methods for withdrawing the senses, but we will deal with two here that are basic techniques used in Yoga practice. The first of these is called the anal lock. It is a useful technique for concentrating on the inner environment and thus diverting one's attention from the outside world. Having completed the necessary preliminary of seating yourself, practising Pranayama, and sounding the OM, you are now ready to turn your attention inward to the region at the base of the spine. Here, in this anatomical site, lies the four-petalled lotus of the Muladhara Chakra. The outer visible or exoteric counterpart of this chakra is formed by the buttocks, the sacrum region, and the perineum. In the diagram, you will notice that the buttocks divide a circle into four quarters forming a pattern similar to its etheric counterpart.

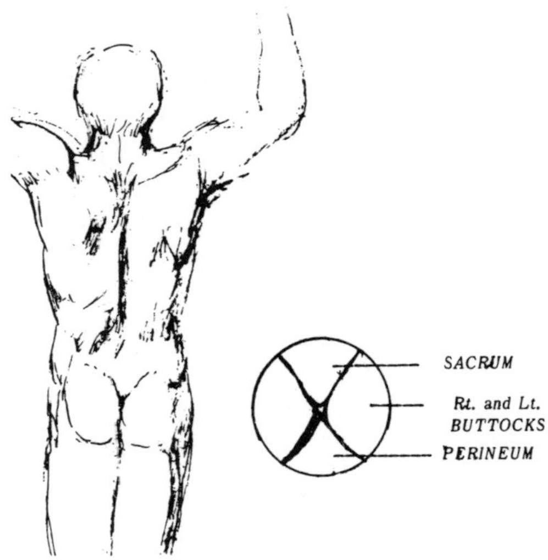

7. The Anal Lock.

Anatomically, the anus, with its rings of muscles (external and internal anal sphincters) is very much like the seated serpent Kundalini and is, in fact, the physical counterpart of kundalini.

The occult law is 'Energy follows thought'. Therefore, by focusing your attention at the base of the spine in the anal lock position, you will be directing the energies of the Ajna Chakra to the Muladhara Chakra. The cave or uterus at the base of the spine will be entered by the light or seed thought of your consciousness; herein lies a hint. The anal lock, called Mulabandha, is performed by first inhaling and then holding the breath while external and internal sphincter muscles are tightly contracted. This action of contracting the anus keeps your attention inside you. Next raise your attention to the solar plexus region and perform the navel lock or stomach lock (Uddiyana Bandha) by drawing the abdomen up and in. This is done at the same time that the anal lock is executed.

Then raise your attention to the space between the eyebrows and perform the frontal gaze by turning the eyeballs inwards and upwards. Hold the locks while retaining the breath to capacity, i.e., as long as it is comfortable, then exhale and release the locks. Perform this exercise several times for a period of five minutes. The attention necessary to hold your eyes inwards and upwards will keep your attention there inside of you. But remember to practice the eye exercises for at least two weeks prior to commencing this stage of the meditation procedure to prevent stiffness of the eyeball muscles.

Eventually you will find, after some months' practice, that you have been able to hold the screen of your mind free of thoughts for some minutes. If you get no further than this, you will have done well because you will have provided higher consciousness than your own with a fertile bed in which they may plant their divine seed thoughts; not the least of these Beings will be your own Higher Self.

Savasana (Corpse Pose)

The ability to relax oneself at will plays an important part in the technique of withdrawing the senses. In the preceding method, the body was automatically being relaxed by alternately contracting and releasing the sphincter muscles. Other muscles were being tensed and relaxed in the process, thus bringing about a total relaxation. Savasana, meaning corpse pose, is a posture in Hatha Yoga, and is performed at the conclusion of a series of postures. Its usefulness lies in the fact that you learn to relax the body as a unit and give in completely to the force of gravity. It is important to master this stage before attempting Yoga Nidra, which is a more advanced technique of relaxation and more difficult to execute unless you have first mastered the corpse pose.

Technique of Savasana

As Savasana is always done in a supine position, lie on your back on a blanket or mat. Take a deep breath and hold it, while simultaneously squeezing and tensing the whole body; then exhale and relax. Repeat this process several times. Then spread your feet apart slightly, with the arms resting next to the body, palms up, and let your body go. Let the legs, the trunk, the arms, the shoulders, the neck, and the head lie completely abandoned and still. Feel the sense of heaviness and relaxation all over the body, part by part, beginning with the feet.

As you bring your attention to the feet, feel the sense of repose, stillness, and heaviness gradually creeping up along the calves, the shins, the knees, the thighs, the hips, and the waist, loosening up all the muscles and tissues. The whole area from the waist to the tips of the toes is utterly abandoned and still. Next feel the trunk, the shoulders, and the arms. Let them lie perfectly still, heavy, and abandoned. Feel the loosening up of all the muscles and tissues in the upper part of the body; the arms rest as if detached from the body limp and heavy. Next feel the neck, the throat, and the head, relaxing all the muscles and tissues in this area. Now feel the whole body; it should be extremely heavy, accompanied by a feeling of deep relaxation.

To deepen your relaxation and to enhance concentration

and visualization, you may perform the following exercise, called polarization. On a slow, even inhalation visualize positive, pranic sun energy, warm and golden yellow in colour being drawn through the top of the head down through the body and out of the soles of your feet. Then, on a slow, even exhalation, visualize negative, pranic moon energy, cool and blue in colour being drawn up through the soles of the feet, through the body and out of the top of the head. Synchronize the breath, visualization, and sensation of energy flow. As you perform this exercise, try to feel the passage of these energies sweeping the body. When concentration has been mastered in this practice, you will begin to feel a distinct electric current passing through the body. The polarization exercise may be practised from 5 to 15 minutes along with Savasana.

Yoga Nidra (Yoga Sleep)

The word Yoga Nidra means Yoga sleep, i.e., putting the body to sleep by means of concentration, but remaining awake and aware at the centre between the eyebrows. In this advanced step, you are going to rotate your consciousness through the body, consciously relaxing any part of the body that is focused on by mentally willing a state of heaviness and relaxation.

Again, remember that you have seated yourself, practised pranayama, and sounded your mantras. You then proceed to withdraw the senses by focusing your attention on each of the following zones of the body for half a minute each. The areas are as follows: feet, shins, calves, knees, thighs, buttocks, abdomen, stomach, chest, spine, hands, arms, neck, head, and face. Focus on each area by concentrating your awareness of that area, mentally will a state of heaviness and relaxation there. Then go on to the next area and repeat the procedure. Go over the body repeatedly until you are so relaxed you fall into a state of Yoga Nidra. All of the foregoing procedures are designed to bring about an altered state of consciousness, along with an eventual slowing down of the rhythmic pattern of the brainwaves into a pattern called the 'alpha state'.

15

Concentration and Meditation

The five preceding stages or limbs are designated to eliminate the various sources of disturbance to the body and mind and to prepare the meditator for the final stages of Dharana concentration, Dhyana, sustained concentration, and Samadhi, the superconscious experience; these are called the internal limbs of Yoga. The previous five stages are really preliminary steps to bring the mind and senses under control. Yama and Niyama eliminate the disturbances caused by uncontrolled emotions and desires, while Asana eliminates the disturbances arising from the physical body. Disturbances caused by the irregular or insufficient flow of Prana in the vital sheath are eliminated by Pranayama. And finally, the major source of disturbance coming through the sense organs and producing impressions on the mind is removed with the practice of Pratyahara. It is only when these conditions have been properly observed that the successful practice of the last three stages is possible.

In Dharana, concentration, there are two essential elements of utmost importance: focus of the mind and visualization. In Dharana, the focus of the mind on a single object is interrupted a number of times as the attention is deviated from the object of concentration, and the meditator gently brings it back to the object. But in Dhyana, the focus of the mind is uninterrupted, and there is a steady flow of attention to the object of concentration. This step is often likened to the pouring of oil from one vessel to another in a steady, unbroken stream.

Alpha, Beta and Theta

Earlier, we mentioned that the five preliminary steps to meditation bring about an altered state of consciousness along with a change in the brain-wave pattern. This pattern of the waking state, called the beta wave, is registered on the polygraph machine as short waves; while in a relaxed state, the brain-wave pattern changes to a slower, longer rhythm called alpha. When a deep state of relaxation is reached, the brain-wave pattern changes to a rhythm that is slower and longer than either the alpha or beta pattern; this wave is called theta. If an electroencephlagraph (EEG machine) were attached to your head during meditation, you would find that you would be going in and out of the alpha state, i.e., from beta, to alpha and back again; then as you relaxed more deeply, theta waves would appear between the alpha and beta waves. The use of the EEG machine only gives a partial indication of what is transpiring in meditation. What it does is simply to measure the length of the brain-wave and its amplitude or strength. It does not measure or record the interior experiences because these are of a subjective nature. All it does is record what is occurring in the physical brain, but not what is happening in the subtle vehicles However, it may give a hint as to what may be happening in Dhyana, sustained concentration.

Most individuals, when they sit down to meditate, are only reaching Dharana, concentration, and not really doing that very well. This is shown on the EEG machine by the fact that most individuals go in and out of alpha many times during their meditation period; in other words they are not able to *sustain* alpha. Also the amplitude of wave of most individuals measures about 40 on a scale from 1 to 100.

However, when trained meditators, such as Yogis and Zen Buddhists are tested, the EEG machine shows that they are able to sustain alpha in meditation and to increase the amplitude of the wave so that it measures 100. Obviously, they are reaching states of consciousness that an untrained meditator is unable to achieve, even after months of training. In other words, what is happening in the case of the trained meditator is that he is reaching the state of Dhyana, sustained concentration, in which the alpha state is sustained without interruption and the amplitude of wave is increased, and this is what is being recorded by the EEG machine. To be able to sustain alpha and to increase the amplitude of the wave one needs to practise visualization exercises over a long period of time and to learn to focus the mind by the use of the will. In other words, we need to develop the function of will in order to focus the mind and to sustain alpha. The practice of esoteric disciplines and of meditation develops the will.

Space Between Thoughts

It must be remembered that meditation occurs in the space between thoughts. No matter how lovely and lofty your thoughts may be, this is not meditation. When the threshold between Pratyahara and Dharana has been reached, it is easy to fall asleep. Therefore, in order to prevent precipitation into the unconscious, it is necessary to concentrate on a form or symbol, bringing it into such clear focus that one fuses with it. Place a symbol in the space between your thoughts and follow that symbol to its source, to its archetype.

In Dharana, there are two things we can concentrate on in the region of the brow: firstly, an image of an object, such as a rose, or a symbol placed there by a process of visualization; or secondly, a concept of formless structure like Truth, Beauty, or Goodness, or something more specific like peace, compassion, or the Brotherhood of Man. In the first instance, the ability to visualize is necessary; in the second, the mind is held pure and clear whilst the higher mind contemplates the concept. As the world of causes is reached with the higher mind, they will be reflected on to the clear mirror of the lower mind. While the first path may be said to be an active one, the second is a passive one, but both lead to true meditation. Again, it should be emphasized that in both instances, meditation only comes when all connection with the lower vehicle is broken.

Many of us have no difficulty in focusing the mind on outward objects, like the print of a book or the stamen of a flower. This is excellent practice, but true meditation is not possible using an object for focus which lies outside the body. It is, of course, recommendable to practise concentrating on objects outside the body as a preliminary to concentration on something inside the body. We must, therefore, learn to concentrate on something 'inside' the body rather than outside the body, and in order to do this we must create in mental substance something we can focus on. This process is called visualization. We must create an image by visualizing it at the centre between the eyebrows.

Right and Left Brain Orientation

In his book *Seeing with the Mind's Eye*, Dr Mike Samuels points out that most formal education does not promote visual imagery because its main focus lies in goal-oriented verbal thought which is a left hemisphere activity of the brain. In most schools, art is a minor subject and more prestige is accorded to the science and math. courses. Psychologists have discovered that specific areas of the brain deal with different thought processes. The right hemisphere, which controls the left side of the body, is primarily responsible for orientation in space, artistic endeavour, crafts, body image, and recognition of faces. The left hemisphere, which controls the right side of the body, is predominantly involved with analytical logical thinking, especially in mathematical and verbal functioning. Thus, the right hemisphere is thought to be responsible for dreams, altered states of consciousness, and intuition.

It has been found that people who are left-brain oriented do not do well in meditation or in areas involving intuitive thinking or artistic endeavours. Hence, it is recommended that methods of training the right hemisphere of the brain will help to bring about altered states of consciousness necessary for the mystical experience. Psychologists, like Robert Ornstein, who is a research psychologist at the University of California, believe that the right hemisphere of the brain can be strengthened by various means, such as concentration exercises involving the visualization of geometric shapes, learning crafts, and working with dreams. It is also felt that the visualization process helps to de-automize ordinary thinking. If we are left-brain oriented, we tend to operate with ordinary linear consciousness most of the time, and our educational system tends to emphasize this type of consciousness. The right hemisphere deals with visual, intuitive, non-linear thought.

Visualization

For most of us who are left-brain oriented, visualization is a difficult process. Often the student is told to visualize something, and he does not know how this should take place or just how clearly he ought to see everything. The explanation that the pictures are similar to those in memory is of no help. At the moment when one tries to remember even the most familiar face, it can happen that parts seem to vanish or everything is blurred, or there is a complete blank in the mind. Of course, when one reaches Dharana, it is hoped that one has some degree of proficiency in visualizing an object. Therefore, in order to be able to visualize when we reach the stage of concentration, it is necessary to practice strengthening the visualization process by a variety of methods.

Training in Observation

An important step in training the mind for visualization is the method of observation, that is, active, alert seeing. Generally, we do not register in our awareness much of our everyday environment because of various screening mechanisms in our make-up. For example, when we walk into a room that we have never seen before, we don't often take note of such things as the colour of the walls or the arrangement of the furniture, or even of the kind of furniture that is in the room, unless it is something spectacular.

The same is true of the street you live in. Although you

have, no doubt, walked down your street many times, if someone should ask you to describe the houses or the scenery there, many of the details would escape you. What you must do is to deliberately train yourself to become aware of your surroundings. For example, when you go into a room for the first time, close you eyes for a few seconds and discover how many objects in the room you can recall. Do this whenever you enter any room or any place new to you. Another exercise in observation is to visualize a room that you are familiar with. At first, visualize the broad outline of the room; then later the details will come. Once you have managed this, visualize yourself walking all around the room, noting the details. Check the accuracy of your visualization by noting the objects that you failed to include in your visualization.

Perform the observation exercise with colours that you see. Look at a colour, then close your eyes and try to see it. Do this again and again with various colours. You may either demand a colour, or you may gently coax it into the mind. It may well take months before you succeed, but once you do, the next step is to shape the colour into geometric patterns, such as a square, a circle, or a triangle. Try drawing the shape on a piece of coloured construction paper and cutting it out; then paste it on a neutral background. Next, look at the coloured shape, then close your eyes and try to visualize it. Keep working at this exercise each day until you are proficient at it; then try visualizing two shapes at once. Make note of any special difficulties, as these notes will be useful to you as a record of your progress.

Visualization in Three Dimensions

It is important to see only what you want to visualize. If for example, the circle you are visualizing becomes distorted, moves about, or increases or decreases in size while you are visualizing it, then you have not yet obtained sufficient control. Once proficiency has been obtained with simple geometric shapes in colour, start training yourself to see it in three dimensions: a cube, a pyramid, a sphere. Try viewing it from different angles, changing your perspective so that you view it from above, from below, from the side, etc. Physically looking at an object from different points of view will help you to visualize an internal object from such a vantage point.

For example, an exercise which involves rapidly shifting viewpoints will be helpful in this respect. Procure an apple. Now, look at the apple as though you were going to eat it, imagining how it tastes as you bite into it. Next, imagine that you are a worm eating your way through the apple. How does the apple appear to you from this point of view? Now imagine you are an artist ready to paint a picture of an apple. Become aware of the colour of the apple, the texture, and the light that is striking the apple. All of these views will put the apple in a different perspective. This shifting of perspectives with other things in your everyday life will give you an expanded awareness of your surroundings.

Training in the ability to see external objects is a basic requirement in the ability to visualize internal objects. Working in art media, such as painting, drawing, photographing, and sculpturing also assists one in training to see external objects. This kind of training, in turn, develops the skill necessary for visualization, that is, seeing objects internally with the mind's eye.

The technique of visualization is not confined to visual images only, but includes a composite of mental impressions which have been received through the other senses as well. Thus you should imagine the feel of velvet, the taste of chocolate, the smell of perfume, the sound of a waterfall. When you visualize a room that you are familiar with, include sounds, odours, textures, and tastes, together with the visual impression.

Tratakam (The Gaze)

Tratakam is an important Yogic practice for developing concentration, and in Raja Yoga it serves as a preparation for Dharana. It consists of steadily gazing at any fixed object for a period of time. Tratakam is the best exercise for retaining a symbol or form in meditation when, in the state of Pratyahara, one would otherwise lose consciousness. It should be mentioned here that Tratakam is practised as a preparation to cross the threshold between Pratyahara and Dharana, and should not be performed for more than twenty minutes. Some of the objects used for Tratakam are a candle flame, a black dot, a symbol, the rising sun, sky or water, crystal, your own shadow, mirror, one of the four elements, one of the chakras, a yantra or a mandala.

The use of the black dot and the candle flame are the usual methods for practising Tratakam. When performing Tratakam with a black dot, it should be fixed on the wall. When doing Tratakam on the candle flame, concentrate on the glowing point at the top of the wick. When your eyes begin to water or feel strained, close them immediately. The eyes should be relaxed, and not straining, so the aim is to keep them open and relaxed as long as possible without blinking. Then close your eyes and focus on the retinal image.

To gaze at the rising sun, as in Tratakam, and to close your eyes and see the retinal image, brings in the rays of Will and Power and stimulates the Will Ray Chakras. To practice Kumbhaka, breath retention, as you gaze at the sun, stimulates the vagus nerve which acts as a receptor to the Solar Fire and transmits it to the tissues within the body. To close your eyes and visualize the sun within yourself increases and extends your ring-pass-not and stimulates the heart chakra.

Concentration of the Chakras

Concentration may be performed by visualizing the appropriate yantra (geometric design) and colour, while sounding the Bija Mantra (syllable) for the appropriate chakra. Reference to the Chakra Chart provides a clear description of the symbolic representations of each chakra. In addition, reference to the diagram entitled Tattva Yantras provides a clear picture of the symbolical representation of each chakra through its Tattva or element. It is suggested that you make models of these yantras using coloured construction paper and mounting them on a black background. A convenient size for the symbol is 3 or 4 inches square. The

TATTVA YANTRAS

Muladahara
Yellow

Svadhisthana
Silver

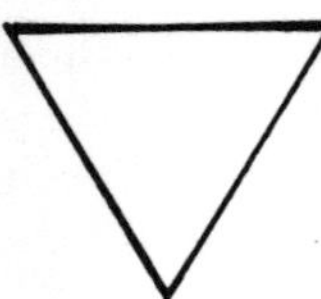

Manipura
Red

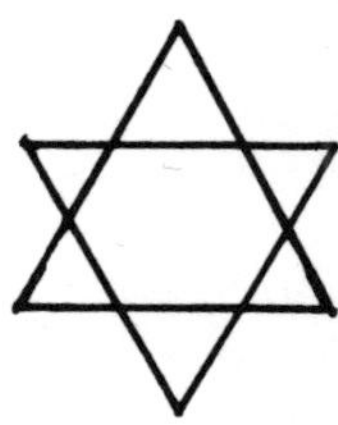

Anahata
Blue

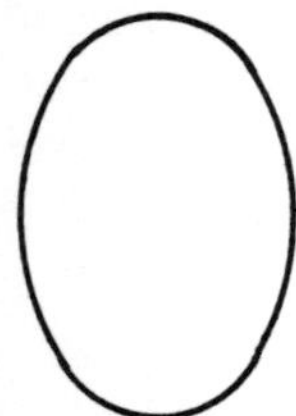

Vishuddha
Violet or Indigo

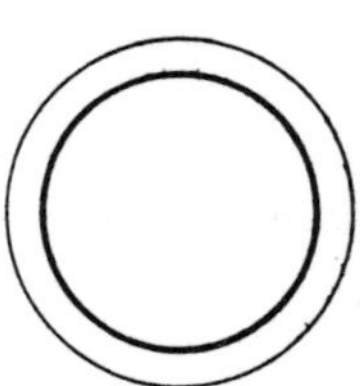

Ajna
Brilliant Yellow

Sahasrara
Scintillating White

result is a set of symbols that may be used in the practice of Tratakam.

To begin your practice, place the yantra before you with the lighted candle to one side so that the diagram is illumined. Start with the Tattva Yantra of the Muladhara Chakra, placing the yellow square before you. Practice Tratakam by fixing your gaze on it, audibly intoning the syllable Lam. Do this for 3 to 5 minutes, attempting to occupy your mind completely with the yellow square and the seed syllable. Then close your eyes and mentally visualize the yellow square while silently repeating the mantra. Finally, move the symbol into its appropriate spot on the spine. In this case, visualize the yellow square at the base of the spine. In the beginning, work with one yantra each day for about 10 minutes. Later, you may dispense with the outward concentration, and perform internal concentration on all seven of the chakras at one sitting.

Symbols

Eventually, for your meditation, select a symbol of occult importance, like the five-pointed star, which is the symbol of the Hierarchy, and focus on it in the Ajna Chakra. Learn to visualize symbols and to focus on them. You may also use the pictures of the Masters for meditation. When you have visualized the image and it is sufficiently clear, bring all your attention to bear upon the most pregnant part of the visualized pattern, the centre of the circle, the eyes of the Master, the tip of the budding rose. What you visualize can come to life whether it is an occult symbol, or whether it is the face of a Master. The eyes will suddenly come alive. You will see compassion and the qualities of the human soul within those glorious eyes.

Meditation Theme

Here is an example of how to concentrate on the pregnant part of what is visualized. The following meditation theme is to be used during the stage called Dharana (concentration). Remember to select your meditation theme before you seat yourself and proceed with the meditation procedure until you arrive at the stage between Pratyahara (withdrawal of the senses) and Dharana (concentration). Now focus your attention at the Ajna Centre. Imagine that you are about to take a voyage, by any means you wish, across a body of water which is a sea about the size of the Mediterranean. The water is a deep indigo blue. Your destination is an island set in the middle of this sea.

It is a lovely, green island with green grass right down to the water. You are on the island now, and above you on a mountain top is a beautiful marble castle with four towers. Before you stretches a path leading to the top of the mountain, and so you begin to climb up the mountain. When you arrive, the gates to the castle swing open, and you pass inside to find yourself standing in the courtyard. In the middle of the courtyard there is a round pool with clear, limpid water. The blue sky is gloriously reflected in the pool, and in the centre of the pool is a lovely lotus with white petals and green leaves. In the opened lotus, right in the centre, there is a jewel of great lustre. Focus on the jewel.

Let us examine the process involved in this meditation theme. You have visualized coloured patterns, and have not only visualized, but you have come right to the central point of importance, which is the jewel in the lotus, in the pool, in the courtyard, of the castle on the green island in the blue ocean. That is what is meant by focusing on what is visualized.

The Pyramid Meditation Theme

Here is a variation of the preceding theme. Again, you have reached the stage in meditation between withdrawal of the senses and concentration and you focus your attention at the brow centre. Once more, you are going to take a journey across a body of water by whatever means you wish. Imagine that you are travelling across a blue-green sea...Your destination is a desert...You are now in the desert, and in the distance you see three pyramid shapes...Your destination is one of these three pyramids. As you approach it, the pyramid grows in size until you are standing before it, a towering, mysterious edifice.

There are seven steps, each in a colour of the rainbow. As you step on each one of them, feel yourself immersed in that colour. The colours of the steps are red, orange, yellow, green, blue, indigo, and violet. Take time to feel the vibration of each colour. When you reach the topmost step, feel a shower of white light flooding you. Before you stands an open door which you will now enter. Once inside, you will be given a symbol which is meaningful to you. Focus on the symbol. A variation of the above is to see your Master standing at the open door.

Door to the Kingdom of Heaven

Focusing on what is visualized takes you to the gate of the kingdom of heaven. You have as it were, created the door to that kingdom by visualizing. You have visualized the door, whether it is a lotus or the face of a Master, makes no difference. You have, as it were, the handle of the door in your grasp, and you focus on the handle of the door. The focus is the act of turning the handle and going inwards. You have now achieved *two* of the *three* prerequisites for the superconscious experience. You have approached the door to the Kingdom of God through visualization of the symbol, and you have your hand on the handle of the door, achieved through focus of the mind.

You now need a third factor to complete the entry and that is energy or power, and for this you use the bellows breath, but it must come reflexly to you. By using all three factors simultaneously, visualization, focus, and breathing, you will storm the kingdom of heaven. Remember, visualize a sacred symbol, focus on the part that is the most pregnant with meaning, and breathe. Each of these factors, when co-ordinated to any extent, brings the opening of the three related chakras in the head centre and the opening of the Third Eye. And when meditation, study of the occult classics, and service to humanity, are part of a student's regime they also open the head centres.

Meditation	**Visualization —**	**Sahasrara Chakra**
Study of the Occult Classics	**Focus —**	**Ajna Chakra**
Service to Humanity	**Breathing —**	**Alta Major Chakra**

However, it is a Herculean task to achieve a synthesis of visualization, focus, and breathing. It is like standing astride three raging horses with the reins tightly grasped. You will struggle with each one of these, but you will not succeed without the help of the Masters. However, if you will serve them, if you will sacrifice yourself for humanity, if you will meditate again and again, day in and day out, without seeking results and rewards, they will help you fight your way to the Light. They will begin to provide you with one of these three factors or two of them, but never three; you must provide one.

This does not mean that no good is obtained until the final moment is achieved. There are many views before the supreme view from the mountain top is reached. Every single effort makes the end, in this life or another, more certain and brings it closer. The path of heaven is made of the stuff of heaven, and the stuff of heaven is of such things as love, compassion, joy, and wisdom. The practice of these along the secret path builds the Antakarana, the golden thread between personality and Soul.

The mere acts of breathing, concentrating, and visualizing do not on their own bring us to the next kingdom, for the kingdom of the Soul is not populated merely by those who can breathe, visualize, and concentrate all at once. However, it is populated by those who can truly meditate, and meditation comes only to those who have incorporated certain qualities into their natures and know by experience what is meant by composure, harmlessness, compassion, and spiritual aspiration. Even spiritually equipped, we still enter that kingdom as children, knowing little about our new environment, and consequently, seeing and understanding much only in distortion.

Seek not, Oh twice-blessed One, to attain the spiritual essence before the mind absorbs. Not thus is wisdom sought. Only he who hath the mind in leash, and seeth the world as in a mirror can be safely trusted with the inner senses. Only he who knoweth the five senses to be illusion, and that naught remaineth save the two ahead, can be admitted into the secret of the Cruciform transposed.

The path that is trodden by the Server is the path of fire that passeth through his heart and leadeth to the head. It is not on the path of pleasure, nor on the path of pain that liberation may be taken nor that wisdom cometh. It is by the transcendence of the two, by the blending of pain with pleasure, that the goal is reached, that goal that lieth ahead, like a point of light seen in the darkness of a winter's night. That point of light may call to mind the tiny candle in some attic drear, but – as the path that leadeth to that light is trodden through the blending of the pairs of opposites – that pin-point, cold and flickering, groweth with steady radiance till the warm light of some blazing lamp cometh to the mind of the wanderer by the way.

Pass on, O Pilgrim, with steady perseverance. No candle is there nor earth lamp fed with oil. Ever the radiance groweth till the path ends within a blaze of glory, and the wanderer through the night becometh the child of the sun, and entereth within the portals of that radiant orb.[2]

[2] *A Treatise on White Magic (From an Ancient Scripture)* by Alice A. Bailey, Lucis Trust 1934.

BIBLIOGRAPHY

BAILEY, ALICE *Letters on Occult Meditation* Lucis Trust, N.Y., 1922. *The Light of the Soul* Lucis Trust, N.Y., 1927. (Commentary on the Yoga Sutras of Patanjali) *A Treatise on Cosmic Fire* Lucis Trust, N.Y., 1925. *A Treatise on the Seven Rays* Vol. IV Lucis Trust, 1953. *A Treatise on White Magic* Lucis Trust, 1934

BAKER, DR DOUGLAS *Anthropogeny* 'Little Elephant', London, 1975. *Jewel in the Lotus*, Vol. I 'Little Elephant' London, 1974. *Meditation* Vol. II 'Little Elephant', London, 1975. *The Opening of the Third Eye* Aquarian Press, London, 1977. *The Powers Latent in Man* Aquarian Press, London, 1977. *The Psychology of Discipleship* 'Little Elephant', London, 1976. *The Spiritual Diary* 'Little Elephant', London, 1977.

BAKER & HANSEN *In the Steps of the Master* 'Little Elephant', London, 1977.

BLAVATSKY, H.P. *Key to Theosophy* Theosophical University Press, Calif., 1946. *The Secret Doctrine* ibid. 1970.

BRENNAN, J.H. *Astral Doorway* Aquarian Press, London, 1971. *Experimental Magic* Aquarian Press, London, 1972.

BUCKE, DR M. *Cosmic Consciousness* E.P. Dutton, N.Y., 1969.

COUKOULIS, PETER *Guru, Psychotherapist and Self* DeVorss, Calif., 1976.

DEROPP, R. *The Master Game* Delta, N.Y., 1968.

EASYCOTT, M. *The Silent Path* Weiser, N.Y., 1969.

GIBRAN, K. *The Prophet* A. Knopf, N.Y., 1923.

HITTLEMAN, R. *Yoga: The 8 Steps to Health and Peace* Dearfield Pub., N.Y., 1975.

JYOTIRMAYANANDA, S. *Concentration and Meditation* Miami, Florida, 1971. *Meditate the Tantric Yoga Way* E.P. Dutton, N.Y., 1973.

LEADBEATER, C.W. *The Chakras* Theosophical Pub. House, Wheaton, III, 1927.

LILLY, DR JOHN *The Centre of the Cyclone* Bantam Books, N.Y., 1972.

MERRELL-WOLFF, F. *Pathways Through to Space* Julian Press, N.Y., 1973.

MISHRA, RAMMURTI *Fundamentals of Yoga* Anchor Books, N.Y., 1974.

MUMFORD, J. *Psychosomatic Yoga* Weiser, N.Y., 1974.

OSBORN, ARTHUR, *Expansion of Awareness* Wheaton, III, 1961.

OUSPENSKY, P.D. *A New Model of the Universe* Vintage Books, 1971.

DE PURUCKER, G. *Occult Glossary* Theosophical Press, Calif., 1972.

RICHARDSON, A. *An Introduction to the Mystical Qabalah* Aquarian Press, London, 1974.

SAMUELS, MIKE & NANCY *Seeing with the Mind's Eye* Random House, N.Y., 1975.

SCHUL & PETTIT *The Psychic Power of Pyramids* Fawcett, Greenwich Conn., 1976.

TAIMNI, I.K. *Science of Yoga* Theosophical Pub. House, Wheaton, III., 1961.

TOBEN, BOB *Space, Time and Beyond* E.P. Dutton, N.Y., 1975.

WEED, JOSEPH *Wisdom of the Mystic Masters* A. Thomas, Northamptonshire, 1978.

YOGANANDA *Autobiography of a Yogi* Self Realization, Calif., 1959.